GOING UP, GOING DOWN

AUP STUDIES IN CULTURAL AND SOCIAL HISTORY, 2
SERIES EDITORS: CAROLINE DALEY AND DEBORAH MONTGOMERIE

Going Up, Going Down

THE RISE AND FALL OF THE DEPARTMENT STORE

HELEN B. LAURENSON

AUCKLAND UNIVERSITY PRESS

First published 2005
Reprinted 2006, 2008

Auckland University Press
University of Auckland
Private Bag 92019
Auckland
New Zealand
www.auckland.ac.nz/aup

ISBN 1 86940 341 X
ISSN 1176-9882

Publication is assisted by the History Group, Ministry for Culture and Heritage.

COVER DESIGN: Base Two
FRONT COVER IMAGE: Window display in the DIC, Christchurch.
BACK COVER IMAGES: Beath's department store, corner Colombo and Cashel Streets, in 1960, and
being outfitted with a school uniform in a Christchurch department store, possibly the DIC, c.1960.
PHOTOGRAPHS: F. E. MCGREGOR (FRONT, BACK RIGHT) AND GREEN AND HAHN (BACK RIGHT).
1982.122.5, 1988.314.4 AND 1982.122.7, CANTERBURY MUSEUM.

Printed by Astra Print Ltd, Wellington

CONTENTS

AUP STUDIES IN CULTURAL AND SOCIAL HISTORY

Edited by Caroline Daley and Deborah Montgomerie, this series
is a forum for rethinking key aspects of New Zealand's past in a lively
and accessible way. Generously illustrated and extensively researched,
the books capture the mood of times past while also asking why
New Zealand history matters and how it should be written.

ACKNOWLEDGEMENTS

I dedicate this book to Eric, who has lovingly and unfailingly encouraged me in my work, and virtually all my enthusiasms – apart from department-store shopping. I acknowledge the heritage of my grandmother Sadie, who, early in her brief life, worked in Ballantynes to provide for her widowed mother and eight younger sisters and brothers; and her daughter, my mother, Lyndall, who introduced me as a child to the delights of department stores. I record with appreciation my brother Ian's interest in my research until his death in 2002; and the loving support of my children, Sarah, Matthew and Anna and their families.

I am most grateful for the vision and encouragement of Dr Caroline Daley and Dr Deborah Montgomerie, who have cheerfully assisted me throughout this journey with understanding and wisdom. To all Elizabeth Caffin's team at Auckland University Press, I express my warmest appreciation for their work, with special thanks to Anna Hodge and Katrina Duncan for their expertise, friendly help, and sound advice.

My thanks, too, to the library staff at the Auckland War Memorial Museum, the staff of the Auckland City Library, particularly in the Special Collections Department, the University of Auckland Library staff, especially those in the Microtext Room, Christchurch Public Library, Canterbury Museum Research Centre, Alexander Turnbull Library, Archives New Zealand, Fletcher Challenge Archives, the Hocken Library, and Radio NZ Sound Archives.

I acknowledge all those individuals whose generous sharing of their time and expertise, photographs and stories, information or hospitality, has so enriched this project: Jack Baker, Bryan Boon, Ian Brailsford, Bryan Burton, Joyce Busfield, William Caughey, Joyce Dey, Fiona de Jardin, Russell English, Gabrielle Fortune, Janet Foster, Jane Garrett, Jeanette Grant, Gail Griffin, Jean Howe, Mavis Jaggar-Smith, Angela Lassig, Ross Lee, Evan Lewis, Clyth MacLeod, Lisa Martens, Robert Milne, Brian O'Connor, Blair Parkes, Kirsten Paterson, Gwen Petch, Daphne Pilaar, Mary Pilkington, Wendy Rhodes, Frank Rogers, Yvonne Sanders, Narelle Scollay, Natalie and Bert Taplin, together with all those unnamed others who have helped in so many ways. My warmest thanks to all.

GOING DOWN

When you go into a big store, you will find an escalator
Which by some Victorians is often called a lift.
There's usually a pretty girl inside the elevator,
Who tells you what's on every floor in case you go adrift.
Starting in the basement that's where there really are things;
Ma gains bargains and doesn't find it hard
To buy a piece of something at three and three three farthings,
Shop-soiled articles and remnants by the yard.

Up in the lift, is it ever going to stop
Till it gets to the top, top, top, top, top?
Top floor — material for sofa, chair or curtain,
Chintz and cretonne, velveteen and casement,
Going down to fifth floor, fourth floor, third floor,
Second floor, first floor, ground floor, basement, hmm . . .
Going down?

Ground floor — grocery, provender, potatoes,
Fruitery, butchery, fishery and wines,
Also cycles, skates, perambulators,
Haberdashery and hosiery and all the latest lines.
First floor — lingerie and crêpe de chine and charmeuse,
Voile and georgette, stockinette and silk,
Undies for Sundays, nighties and pyjamas,
Chemises that pleases and 'camies' and the ilk.

Back to the lift, is it ever going to stop . . .

Second floor — wireless sets, gramophones, pianos,
Fiddles, flutes and saxophones, complete in leather case.
Also new songs for tenors or sopranos
And lower songs written for contraltos or a bass.
Third floor — model hats, millinery from Paris,
Also on the third floor, every kind of frock or gown;
Not to mention tweed things Donegal and Harris,
Everything a lady wears in country or in town.

Back to the lift, is it ever going to stop . . .

Fourth floor, garden tools, basket chairs, and arbors,
Hose pipes and water cans to make the plants behave.
Also ladies' 'coiffeur' as they never call them barbers,
'Have you an appointment Madam for a water-wave?'
Fifth floor, toy things, dolls of all nations,
Indians from India and Eskimos from Esk;
Also the restaurant with coffee and collations
Which patrons are requested to pay for at the desk.

Back to the lift, is it ever going to stop
Till it gets to the top, top, top, top, top?
Top floor — material for sofa, chair or curtain,
Chintz and cretonne, velveteen and casement,
Going down to fifth floor, fourth floor, third floor,
Second floor, first floor, ground floor, basement, hmm . . .
Street level!

RONALD FRANKAU. PERFORMED BY NORMAN LONG, 'ENTERTAINER AT THE PIANO',
C.1936. COL DO 722, SOUND ARCHIVES/NGA TAONGA KORERO.

Roach's department store in Hastings in the 1920s before its tragic destruction, with the loss of 17 lives, in the 3 February 1931 earthquake. 019263, ALEXANDER TURNBULL LIBRARY, WELLINGTON.

'Where have all the department stores gone, long time passing?' an American entre-preneur recently asked.[1] The focus of an exciting day's shopping in town, department stores once played an important role in the lives of many New Zealanders. Photographs of a bygone era, together with memories that reach back several decades, reveal that the department stores added their own distinctive character to our cities and provincial towns. In each of the main centres one *grande dame* still remains, face-lifted, relatively short in stature, but cherished and elegant, offering shoppers a unique and luxurious experience of colour and style.[2]

Today, though, suburban shopping malls have become the places where due homage is paid to consumerism. No longer a tale of great and busy 'cathedrals of consumption', the story of New Zealand's former department stores comes into sharper relief when considered from the vantage point of the early twenty-first century.[3] It is time to consider their gradual and inexorable journey from a confident position in the mid-1920s, when expansion and consolidation marked their debut as major retailers, to the point where anxieties about their future as large, inner-city or provincial town stores were expressed. Now is the moment to revisit many of those fascinating and many-splendoured places that, in their heyday, drew crowds of men, women and children to enter their doors. Their allure is legendary; their mystique awaits our discovery and exploration.

Colonial New Zealand offered good opportunities for men and women with experience in the drapery trade and a shrewd business sense. The threads of the narratives that tell their stories are often long and colourful, like the skeins of yarn

An early postcard photograph of Brown Ewing's department store in Princes Street, Dunedin (left), with a horse and cart in front. This card is postmarked 16 April 1909.

they sold in their stores. George Low Beath, for instance, served an apprenticeship in the city of Dunfermline, Scotland, and spent a year in Melbourne, before arriving in Christchurch. In 1866, he joined Oscar Kirby in Kirby's small Cashel Street drapery shop, which had opened in 1860. Beath's was destined for a longstanding relationship of friendly rivalry with nearby Ballantynes department store. John Ballantyne, who in 1872 purchased William Pratt's business, had been apprenticed in the drapery trade in Berwick-upon-Tweed. Another who had learned the trade in that same northernmost English port was Thomas Brown. Having arrived in Bluff in early 1863, Brown moved to more prosperous Dunedin in 1865 and was employed in Ross & Glendining's drapery business when that firm moved to manufacturing. Together with Ralph Ewing and John Glendining, Brown took over the store, which opened as Brown, Ewing & Co. in August 1866.[4] In that same year in Dunedin, brothers Alexander and Thomas Inglis, also

Farmers' store on the corner of Hobson and Wyndham Streets showing two of the store's free buses. The new façade designed by Lippincott was not completed until 1937. I. HUNTER.

Scots, set up a small drapery shop. Their ambition to have a store on the main street was realised when the firm moved to a new building in George Street in 1877. Thomas died in 1876, and did not witness the reaching of that promised land, although he had seen branches opened at Port Chalmers, Invercargill and Oamaru.

Among the many storekeepers whose names are fading from memory are those like Kirkcaldie and Stains, which have become household, even national, by-words. Towards the end of 1863 'the latest novelties from the London and Paris market' featured in the first advertisement for drapers John Kirkcaldie and Robert Stains, setting up a small store on Lambton Quay, 'better known to old Wellingtonians as "The Beach"'.[5] Five months later, as harbour reclamation work proceeded, they moved their stock across the road into Waterloo House and, in 1868, to larger premises opened on the corner of Lambton Quay and Brandon Street.

Despite New Zealand's economic depression of the 1880s, these and other firms survived to stand proudly in the ranks of the emerging department stores. In 1884 the Drapery Importing Company of New Zealand Ltd was established in High Street, Dunedin, the first of a number of DIC stores throughout New Zealand. Originally from Germany, founders Bendix Hallenstein and his brothers moved to Dunedin and set up New Zealand's first clothing factory and warehouse, also supplying a chain of stores nationwide under their family name, Hallenstein Bros.

There were others who braved the trading difficulties of the time. George Court arrived in Auckland with his wife Alice and four children (a fifth child, a daughter, was reportedly born on the wharf), as a severe nationwide recession hit the city.[6] He set up 'The Beehive' drapery store on the corner of Liverpool Street and Karangahape Road in 1886.[7] From there, joined by his older brother Fred, he opened a Queen Street branch in June 1889. Also in 1889, a third brother, John Court, with his wife and eight children, left Birmingham to join the firm of Court Bros, drapers and clothiers, of Queen Street and Karangahape Road.

Farmers' Trading Company was an exception to the expanded drapery-shop model of department store development. In 1886, as an infant, Robert A. C. Laidlaw travelled from Scotland to Dunedin, where Robert Laidlaw senior operated hosiery and hardware businesses. In 1909, after working as a travelling hardware salesman for three or four years, young Robert began his own mail-order business, Laidlaw Leeds, in Auckland.[8] This enterprise flourished and was transferred to a newly erected Hobson Street warehouse in April 1914. In 1918 the firm was merged with the Farmers' Union Trading Company, and by 1920 had 29 branches in the Auckland Province, and three factories. In 1919 work began on doubling the size of the mail-order warehouse, which was opened to the public in October 1920 as a department store. An adjoining seven-storey block was completed in 1921, and the company opened an annexe in 1930, enabling their main building to be freed for extra retail space.

Meanwhile, in Christchurch, the persistently entrepreneurial James L. Hay had tried his hand at a variety of occupations. In 1925 he was employed by Ballantynes as an advertising manager; but after being politely informed that his enthusiastic style differed from the firm's traditional image, he left in 1929. With a small investment in the company, he started James Hay's, a subsidiary of Macky Logan Caldwell, an Auckland firm and one of New Zealand's largest manufacturing and wholesale warehousing companies. Shortly after the Wall Street share-market crash of October 1929, the new business commenced trading in Gloucester Street on an inauspicious Friday, 13 December 1929; Hay, a staunch Presbyterian, had no qualms about the date. When Macky Logan Caldwell encountered trading difficulties in 1933, James Hay, nothing daunted, went on to form a public company with Canterbury shareholders.

The buoyant economic climate of the mid-1920s also encouraged an Australian, Lesley Beaumont Miller, to set up in a small shop in Ferry Road in 1926. Miller, who had come to Christchurch from Greymouth, then started a retail outlet and a clothing factory in Strange's building on the corner of Lichfield and High Streets in 1930, even going to the length of buying an Invercargill woollen mill to supply his shop.

These stores, and others like them in cities and towns around New Zealand, developed later than their British, European, American, or Australian counterparts but they experienced growth patterns similar to many overseas department stores. As their trade prospered, they enlarged their premises by acquiring adjacent land for additional plant, added more storeys to their buildings, or moved to other larger and more central sites. It seemed that the larger they grew, the more successful they became. The three-storey corner store on Queen Street and Victoria Street East, Auckland, which became known as John Court Ltd, for instance, had been built by the Direct Supply Company in 1899 after a fire destroyed the Greyhound Hotel. By 1909 John Court had three shops in Queen Street, and ambitions for bigger, consolidated premises on a central site, so bought the freehold of the DSC store in 1910, quitting the other outlets. In 1916, three and a half floors were added to John Court's corner building.

Similarly, James Smith Ltd purchased a block of buildings on the corner of Cuba and Manners Streets in the busy heart of Wellington in 1920 and undertook extensive alterations and renovations.[9] New technology and construction methods and rising land values meant multi-storey structures made financial sense. Notwithstanding the purchase of neighbouring sites by several of the stores in the 1920s, it was often more economic to build upwards than to extend laterally.[10] Most store additions had been completed before 1931, when Napier's disastrous earthquake led to a re-evaluation of New Zealand's codes of building practice. Tragically, 17 people lost their lives when Roach's two-storey department store in Hastings collapsed and was destroyed by fire on 3 February 1931.[11] Neither Blythe's three-storey, ferro-concrete department store, proudly opened on a site in Emerson Street, Napier, in March 1917, nor their earlier adjoining building, survived the massive earthquake and the fire which followed. Yet within a couple of months, Blythe's advertisements for the firm 'founded in 1872, and still confidently facing the future', bravely announced that they had recovered and were back in temporary premises.[12]

Usually family concerns, with the energy and the continuity of management that this implied, department stores established distinct identities, steadily consolidated their businesses and often retained the names under which they had been founded. Occasionally, marriages between members of those families furthered networks of business as well as personal interest. Increasing in size and importance, the stores flourished through the first decades of the twentieth century, in the 'golden age' of

John Court Ltd on the corner of Queen Street and Victoria Street East. This was the former Direct Supply Company store purchased by John Court in 1910. Alterations, including the adding of three floors, were completed in 1916. This photograph would have been taken between those years.

New Zealand department stores. Modern and up to date with fashion, brimming with colour and light, bustling with purposeful shoppers and courteous staff, they were the pivotal centres of interest around which much of the life of cities and towns in New Zealand revolved. They offered a glimpse of the exotic 'other' — the world of the great metropolis.

By the 1920s, New Zealand, with its important shipping links to Australia, Britain and the United States, was up to the mark with major retailing developments overseas. Many New Zealanders had experienced overseas travel in the first two decades of the twentieth century, some for the first time during World War I, and would have seen for themselves the great department stores of London and Paris. They were becoming increasingly familiar with the use of the new American term 'department stores' for the shops they had formerly known as 'emporia'.[13]

Reaching a concise definition of what a department store actually is has been a topic of considerable discussion in the late twentieth century. It has been stated that department stores were 'invented' by the 'revolutionary innovations of [Aristide] Boucicaut', who, with his wife, Marguerite, developed the famous Bon Marché in mid-nineteenth-century Paris. Boucicaut's ideas, which were integral to the operation of nineteenth- and twentieth-century department stores, involved selling large amounts of merchandise at a small mark up, using fixed prices instead of bargaining, offering free access to all, without any obligation to buy, and providing shoppers with the right of exchange or refund for goods bought. Other historians, including the author of the Bon Marché's definitive history, maintain, however, that some of Boucicaut's 'new' initiatives had been already current practice for some years in England and France.[14]

Historians have tried to clarify the combination of features that define department stores, with size and organisational structure as key features. Large retail establishments, they are distinguished by their high level of capitalisation, selling a great range of merchandise within separate departments with their own individual managers and buyers. They operate with centralised functions, including advertising and accounting, mail-order and delivery, and offer an array of services for customers within comfortable, often luxurious settings.[15]

The vertical arrangement of the floors, each one devoted to a different group of departments, was characteristic of most of the stores. In comparison with the size, construction materials, and features of many overseas department stores, New Zealand's structures are relatively modest; yet within the central business districts, department stores, usually several storeys high, stood as significant landmarks, defining and adding to the character of their city or town. From the top floor of Beath's new six-storey building in the heart of Christchurch in 1915, the delights of 'the vista of the far Kaikouras to the north, the snow capped Southern Alps to the West, with foothills, plain and city in the foreground, and the Pacific away to the east' were open to view for Cantabrians, most of whom had been accustomed to life on the level.[16]

In this book, as in department stores, each chapter opens on a different floor. Although the themes of consumption and modernity are continuous throughout, the first three chapters deal with their effect on what were distinct and separate groups of shoppers. Men, women and children responded to the efforts of the stores to woo and retain their custom from the early 1920s until the 1960s by using and enjoying the services they provided, by being entertained by the special features they displayed, and above all, by regularly buying from the variety of quality consumer goods on offer.

In order to place department stores within their context as expressions of consumerism, it is important to examine consumption itself. Chapter Four looks at consumption in its most literal form, food service, rarely given space in the many studies of department stores. A visit to the tearoom provides a taste of the changes apparent in the stores during the period under study.

Definitions of consumers and their attitudes vary greatly. The consumer has been described by Peter Ackroyd as 'one who can only experience the world by the act of ingestion or assimilation'. With consumption expressed 'in terms of processes of commodification, spectatorship, commercial exchanges, and social welfare reforms, processes that involve the desire for and sale, purchase and use of durable and nondurable goods, collective services and images', its definition is wide-ranging.[17] It is an elusive subject of research, resistant to a concise definition, just as one of its symbolic representations, the department store itself, has eluded a single definition.

The growth of consumption is difficult to explain in a convincing way. John Benson, studying changes in the rise of British consumer society over a century, identified three explanations for increasing consumption, 'manipulation', 'emulation' and 'amelioration'.[18] Peter Stearns, too, listed 'manipulation', and added 'fulfillment of social and personal needs', and 'habituation'.[19] The latter might well describe Mrs Emily Poole's daily visit to Farmers' department store, departing from her home in Point Chevalier at the same time each morning and always staying for lunch.[20] Such a pattern

James Smith's corner at night, c.1920s or early 1930s, showing an amazing variety of goods on display.

of commitment over many years demonstrates the engrossing and even addictive experience of being a consumer in such an attractive setting.

While Marxist and left-wing cultural theorists argue that a controlling elite determines the needs and wishes of the population, and others promote theories of 'consumer sovereignty', viewing individuals as controlling agents in the process of consumption, the idea of 'consumer democracy' seems best suited to the New Zealand scene. This notion of consumption as an expression of popular culture is of a fluid and changing process, actively made by the shifting allegiances, formations and agencies of people themselves, and not imposed upon them from without.[21]

'Consumer democracy' is a pragmatic concept, its nature very much akin to those shoppers who chose to make their way into the ground floor of New Zealand's department stores. Chapter One addresses how consumers were attracted into the stores and to what extent, having entered, they were influenced in their patterns of consumption by the gendered arrangement of the ground floor. This floor traditionally offered men the opportunity to shop in what was perceived as a women's world. Men, associated in some theories of a consumer society with the production of goods, rather than as the purchasers and users of them, were consumers too in their own right.

In order to attract customers, it was important to present the widest possible variety of goods available within these large buildings. With efficiency in stock turnover, and the greater scale of department store operations, goods could usually be sold at cheaper prices than in specialist shops. Although prices were maintained at reasonable levels, department stores throughout New Zealand faced problems sourcing a variety of merchandise for their female customers. Within this context, Chapter Two looks at women as shoppers, negotiating their way through issues of fashion and supply.

The phenomenon of the department store has been linked with the enormous increase in the production and availability of manufactured goods, which followed the urbanisation and industrialisation of late-nineteenth-century Western Europe and America. Others have claimed, however, that consumption and the world of goods was a feature of early-modern society and culture.[22] In a study of early consumerism the role of children was traced as they moved from employment within the family to a special place of privileged consumption, usually by others on their behalf. This reflected the aspirations of adults for their offspring in the provision of clothing, goods and education, as well as the needs of the children. Little has been written on children and consumption in relation to department stores. Chapter Three looks at the stores and their relationship with mothers as consumers, together with children as future consumers.

What can the study of department stores add to our understanding of New Zealand culture and society? It has been argued that the less powerful seek consumption as a way of demonstrating and elevating their standing in society. At the end of the nineteenth century, Thorstein Veblen coined the term 'conspicuous consumption', for the apparent spending on valuable goods in order to gain status.[23] Historians attempting to trace the origins of consumer culture in the United States have focused on the last two decades of the nineteenth century as especially significant. Consumption was to become more than a way of providing for one's needs; it was to become a way of understanding one's place in the world.[24] In the late nineteenth century, values of hard work, saving, civic and community responsibility, and a morality based on self-denial, were losing ground in American society. A new cluster of values defined an emerging group of middle-class consumers who had more disposable income, together with an expectation of more leisure time, more spending, and more individual fulfilment.[25] Like America, New Zealand experienced profound changes as it moved into the modern world of the twentieth century. In visiting department stores and hearing the stories of the people who shopped in these large establishments, we can view more closely the impact of some of those changes in New Zealand society and its patterns of consumption; we can also savour some of the attractions of modernity, its style, cut and flair.

The notion of modernity, like consumption, has many definitions. In social and economic terms it has been linked with changes brought about by industrialisation and urbanisation.[26] Erik Olssen applied the concept of 'modernization' to his study of the interrelated changes that occurred in New Zealand in 1890–1940, arguing that the country had been transformed into a modern society by the end of the 1920s. Major social and economic changes have continued to characterise twentieth-century New Zealand. Modernity, with its interest in the present and the future, its concept of leisure, its fascination with the new and its assumption that change is for the better, was an important influence on New Zealand society throughout the years from 1920 to 1960. Arguably, consumer society cannot exist, let alone develop, without a belief in modernity.[27] Not only is modernity inextricably interwoven with change, but, by its very nature, the signs of modernity change with the times. What was modern at the beginning of this period is not necessarily consistent with modernity forty years later.

In 1960, Hay's opened a store in a new suburban shopping centre in Upper Riccarton, Christchurch. A year later, two of the largest of Auckland's department stores, Farmers' and Milne & Choyce, together with chain-store giant, Woolworth's, and the Australian Mutual Provident Society (AMP), signalled their concern to hold their position in the frontline of the retail battle when they bought a block of land from the Auckland Bus Company in New Lynn and built New Zealand's first shopping mall.[28] Free from parking problems, malls were created as shopping centres for rapidly expanding suburban housing developments and were seen as a novel and enlivening trend, already well established in the United States, Britain, Europe and Australia.

Department store shopping in the 1920s, with its service, comfort and amazing selection of goods, its freshly reconstructed buildings with their 'facades of colour, glass

LynnMall shopping centre under construction, August 1963. It was planned that the total floor-space of the mall would be equalled by the area for car-parking. T. W. CURHAM.

and light', was an exciting experience.[29] New Zealand's department stores endeavoured to anticipate changing patterns of consumption and retain their place as agents of modernity. In their quest for potential customers, they targeted men, women and children, drawing them into the heart of their towns and cities to enter these imposing structures, and to savour what was new and modern in the twentieth century. In turn New Zealanders treasured their department stores and enjoyed the many wonderful experiences and services they offered.

This book celebrates the joys and delights of department store shopping as it tracks the gradual movement of the stores from heyday to yesterday. To draw readers into the excitement and expectation of that fascinating progression, it evokes the echoes of those litanies chanted by long-gone, uniformed and gloved lift-attendants, as they performed their duties as acolytes in those 'cathedrals of consumption'. Let us pass through those heavy glass doors, and enter the grand space of the ground floor. Immediately we experience an atmosphere quietly humming with activity, redolent with the perfume of cosmetics, vibrant with colour and promise. We pass counters laden with goods and their smiling, smartly turned-out attendants. We head towards the lifts to catch again that familiar call: 'Ground floor — going up?'

ALL-DAY
FREE MOTOR SERVICE

Our Customers, and Patrons of our
Tea Rooms, are invited to make free
use of the Special Motor 'Bus, which
is now running daily between our
Warehouse and Queen Street, via
Wyndham Street, leaving foot of
Wyndham Street every 5 minutes.

SEE MAP ON OTHER SIDE

**HOURS : Monday to Thursday, 9 a.m. till 5 p.m.
Friday, 9 a.m. till 9 p.m.**

*Why climb the hill when this conveyance is
at your service ?*

FARMERS' UNION TRADING CO. (AUCK) LTD.
Corner Hobson and Wyndham Streets

[SEE OTHER SIDE

Farmers' first free bus in 1922 was a converted truck that could carry 15 passengers.

CHAPTER ONE

Ground Floor — Going Up

'The best department store in the world for us had to be George Court's. Long before I'd seen Macy's and Bloomingdale's, George Court's teemed with people and interesting things', wrote Bob Harvey, remembering with pleasure the bustle and variety of Karangahape Road as it was in his childhood.[1] By the late 1940s, when Bob was a small boy, George Court's, like many other large department stores throughout New Zealand, had experienced years of adversity as well as prosperity. To young Bob, then happily unaware of any major obstacles to successful retailing, this store, like no other, presented a fascinating world of possibility, just a hop, skip and jump away from his home.

Retailers had a difficult time in the years following World War I. A worldwide recession in 1920 and 1921 had threatened plans for the extension of several New Zealand department stores. This economic slump was a result of wartime shortages and high costs. When the accumulation of back orders was filled at the end of the war, an oversupply of goods flooded the stores. Prices often dropped well below replacement value and retailers faced enormous losses in writing down their stock. By the early 1920s, however, stores as widely scattered as Milne & Choyce in Auckland, Arthur Barnett in Dunedin and H. & J. Smith in Invercargill were daring enough to go ahead with ambitious plans for redeveloping their sites. When undertaking such risky ventures, management was increasingly aware of the importance of advertising to bring customers into their stores. For four years Arthur Barnett's customers went on buying while builders worked around or underneath them. In 1921, Milne & Choyce accommodated an Aladdin's Christmas Cave 'amidst the hard stone-like walls and

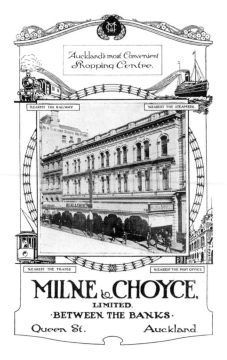

massive columns of an unfinished portion of our new building . . . walk through the Giant's mouth into this delightful hiding place of toys'.[2] Although Milne & Choyce had not finished its reconstruction by 1922, and Farmers' Trading Company was experiencing considerable financial difficulties during 1922 and 1923, department stores throughout New Zealand were beginning to reflect new levels of confidence. Despite past problems and future uncertainties, store entrepreneurs were ready for expansion. Kirkcaldie & Stains recorded a less than successful trading record through the 1920s, but by 1928 was substantially remodelling both the interior and the frontage of its Lambton Quay establishment. Department store development on a grand scale characterised the later years of the decade.

The large, inner-city stores were strategically located at the heart of central business districts, well served by trams and trains, buses and ferries. In the first decade of the twentieth century, electric tram services began in Auckland, Wellington, Christchurch, Dunedin and Wanganui, with Invercargill, Napier, Gisborne and New Plymouth following soon after.[3] In 1904, the DIC in Wellington proudly stated 'All [tram]cars stop here'.[4] From the early 1900s until 1920, tramway services were at their peak of popularity. Thereafter, competition with buses and, later again, with cars, began to affect public transport patterns.

In 1922, New Zealand's first free bus service (initially in a converted truck that could carry up to 15 passengers) transported shoppers from Auckland's Queen Street to Farmers' in Hobson Street.[5] Robert Laidlaw's shrewd provision of free transport channelled customers to his department store from Queen Street and, later, Karangahape Road, encouraging many people to follow a canny and tactical shopping route.[6] Alighting from their tram or bus at Karangahape Road, shoppers walked to Rendell's and nearby George Court's department stores to see the latest goods on offer. From adjacent Pitt Street, free transport operated to bring customers to Farmers' store. After (or instead of) 'doing' Farmers', passengers could board the free bus, which travelled down to the heart of the city, depositing them near Queen Street, at no charge.[7] Those with determination and stamina, who were not already laden with too many packages, could then zigzag along Queen Street to Milne & Choyce, John Court Ltd, and Smith & Caughey's. These three stores, all fronting on to the main street at suitably discrete intervals, were within easy walking distance of each other.

Laidlaw had another strategy to capture the business of those coming into the city by private car. By 1928, he had opened the first free car park for shoppers in Australasia, with spaces for 87 cars. A Farmers' publicity leaflet of the time reassuringly stated: 'When you park here, your mind is free from the fear that you are exceeding the parking limit and that a traffic inspector may have your number'.[8] Shoppers' worries about where to park in the central city are clearly nothing new.

On the face of it, the inner-city stores offered sites with easy access from tram, bus, train, ferry or car as they competed for shoppers' business. In practice they worked together to create separate shopping destinations. The stores' closeness to one another could be advantageous as they sought to complement, match, or exceed each other's efforts in merchandising. The DIC competed with Beath's and Ballantynes in Christchurch as one of 'three in a row' in Cashel Street.[9] Arthur Barnett's foresight in

Kirkcaldie & Stains department store on Lambton Quay in the 1930s, with the
DIC building in close proximity. 015403, ALEXANDER TURNBULL LIBRARY, WELLINGTON.

setting up in George Street in 1903, when Dunedin's retailing hierarchy were perceived as holding court further south in Princes Street, was a successful move, since another large department store, A. & T. Inglis, was already based in that same street, north of the Octagon. The Wellington branch of the DIC first set up business in the 1890s in Cuba Street, where there were several other department stores, but later deserted their ranks and shifted northwards to a site with frontages on Brandon and Panama Streets. At the end of February 1929, success crowned the DIC's moves to reach Lambton Quay when its enormous, six-storey building was opened. It stood as a check to Kirkcaldie & Stains just across the road.

Not entirely dependent on a single cluster of stores, shoppers could always be prevailed upon to venture further in search of a good buy. Location was important, but bargains mattered too. A worker in the DIC Christchurch, recalled 'it was very competitive in those days. Hay's was down the other end [of town]. It was very well thought of.'[10] Armstrong's and Miller's also offered cheaper prices. At the top of Queen Street in Auckland, Karangahape Road, with its 'wide level footpaths, unusually good verandah protection for shoppers . . . and tradition of economical family shopping', was only a short stroll away from the densely settled neighbourhood of workers' cottages in Newton Gully.[11] Similarly, department stores such as C. Smith's, Whitehead & Pears, George & George, and James Smith's, in Cuba Street, Wellington were within walking distance of workers' homes in Te Aro and Brooklyn. Many of these houses in both Auckland and Wellington, together with church and school buildings, were to be swept away by motorway extensions in the 1960s. During the period of this study, however, they accommodated significant communities that supported the pattern of busy retailing nearby. For Bob Harvey, a 'Gully boy', Karangahape Road was virtually his own backyard, a stamping ground shared with all those who might come from further afield to check out the latest 'interesting things' available in town. A large department store like George Court's, with its policy of free entry for all, with no compulsion to buy, was a proud feature of his neighbourhood.

Entering George Court's meant passing a series of stylish and spectacular window displays. Well-lit window-runs were department stores' most powerful advertisements, awakening interest and stimulating stock turnover.[12] Extensive windows on busy road frontages had been a feature of overseas department stores since their establishment in the nineteenth century, and, together with the windows of other commercial and business institutions, dramatically changed the appearance of city streets. Since no

ABOVE: George & Kersley's arcade of windows in their Wanganui store offered a new world of display possibilities for the DIC. 016364, ALEXANDER TURNBULL LIBRARY, WELLINGTON.

OPPOSITE: The DIC bought George & Kersley's 'Economic' drapery shop in Wanganui, famous for its 'beautiful windows'. 015990, ALEXANDER TURNBULL LIBRARY, WELLINGTON.

plate-glass was manufactured in New Zealand, supplies were imported at some cost from Sydney, Britain or Europe.[13] Large shop windows established the credibility, wealth and eminence of firms, and served as '3D catalogues, crammed with goods'.[14] The management of the DIC stores originally frowned on window displays as unnecessary, expensive and damaging to stock, and promoted warehouse-style trading. With the 1920 acquisition of George & Kersley's drapery business in Wanganui, however, the DIC gained a building famous since its 1914 opening as 'the store with the beautiful windows'.[15] From this point, large display windows became a recognised and important feature of DIC department stores and were installed as the firm's buildings were renovated or constructed. Farmers' in Auckland, however, originally conceived as a massive warehouse, never installed large display windows, astutely maintaining there was too little foot traffic passing along either Hobson or Wyndham Streets to justify their existence.

By the 1920s, stores regarded their windows as a retail asset, each vying with the other to present glamorous and artistic displays.[16] Formerly the windows had been jam-packed with as much merchandise as possible; now style and presentation took precedence over cluttered content. Displays were inspired by specialised publications originating in the United States from the turn of the century onwards.[17] In August 1925, with the new street frontage of Milne & Choyce's building completed, staff member

A spectacularly beautiful display of 'Brides of the Ages' in Milne & Choyce's windows in the 1920s. 90.1.48, AUCKLAND WAR MEMORIAL MUSEUM LIBRARY.

John Court's building at night, c.1922. *THE CITY OF ENTERPRISE, 1889–1923* [JOHN COURT LTD], AUCKLAND, 1923.

F. J. Constant visited North America and Canada 'for the purpose of making himself thoroughly acquainted with the most up-to-date methods and schemes of decorating, window dressing, display etc'.[18] Such enterprise paid off. A year later, a newspaper journalist enthused that Milne & Choyce's 'splendid modern windows for the display of goods are used to such artistic effect that thousands of people inspect them daily'.[19]

Brightly lit windows presented tantalising merchandise from around the world to a public then unused to such visual variety outside of a theatre. John Court Ltd had '12 large windows facing Queen Street and Victoria Street which were constantly changed by a staff of six'.[20] Until the mid-1920s, headless models had been used to display garments in Arthur Barnett's Dunedin store. Six glamorous wax figures, designed and made by Pierre Imam in Paris, were imported to grace the store's re-vamped building, and took their place alongside the headless mannequins in elegant window displays.[21] Indeed, one Dunedin historian stated 'the most effective department store displays were in fact found in the windows'.[22] Store windows reinforced links with modernity as they presented a glimpse of things to come, constantly changing with the seasons, and presenting the latest in fashion. At the height of the Great Depression in Christchurch,

Six lifelike wax models from Pierre Imam of Paris provided a dramatic contrast to the previously used headless display forms in Arthur Barnett's store window in 1925. *OTAGO WITNESS*, E6877, HOCKEN LIBRARY.

said to be the worst affected of all the main centres, Ballantynes' displays were 'changed every three days in order to maintain interest with the passing public'.[23]

This ever-changing pageant of modernity faltered when electricity and goods were in short supply. Blackout regulations came into force in the early 1940s, and power cuts, which began during World War II, continued for several years after the end of the war. In autumn 1948, Auckland shoppers were still being reassured: 'In the advent of power cuts M. & C.'s [Milne & Choyce's] auxiliary lighting plant will be in operation. You won't know the difference.'[24] Maintaining high standards of display was difficult. Decorations had to be improvised, refurbished and recycled during the mid-1940s. Teams of window dressers, usually men, worked with determination and ingenuity to overcome the constraints created by import restrictions, shortages of manufactured goods and rationing.[25] There were high expectations as New Zealanders celebrated their first post-war festival in 1945, 'but we haven't had any decorations from overseas; we're still using left-overs from six years ago, we've never had such a difficult Christmas before', sighed one frustrated window-dresser.[26] Christmas display windows were part of the enchantment of the season for children like Bob, as well as for adults of both sexes; as William Leach stated 'through its windows the department store exercised its most magical and immediate external appeal'.[27]

Some could only consume the image. As Leach observed of the goods featured in American displays, 'unless you shatter the window or go in and pay for it, you cannot have it. In such a context, the breaking of glass could easily have become a class act.'[28] The plate-glass windows of department stores did indeed represent the structure of a powerful, capitalist establishment to New Zealand's unemployed workers in the early 1930s. Some department stores, recognising that their high visibility had become a potential liability, took out special insurance against damage to their windows. Although the stores continued their pattern of regular charitable donations, even resorting to gifts in kind when their own finances were under siege during the Depression, spontaneous outbursts of violence revealed a depth of feeling against department store merchants.[29] Rioters, the majority of whom were male, smashed store windows. One newspaper reported that the unemployed 'paid little attention to the windows of banks, mercantile offices or hotels, their purpose evidently being concentrated on shops'.[30] When rioters charged down Queen Street, Auckland on the evening of Thursday, 14 April 1932, they broke all 14 of Smith & Caughey's windows. As they drew near to Milne & Choyce, an assistant hurriedly removed display figures from the windows, the valuable wax models suffering some damage in the process.[31] George Court's and Rendell's windows were also broken in Karangahape Road riots on the night of Friday, 15 April 1932, together with those of many other shops along the stretch of road from Pitt Street to Queen Street.[32] The newspaper report noted that there were more women in the crowd than had been observed in Queen Street the previous night. Karangahape Road's hinterland of working-class housing was no doubt a factor in their presence. Three weeks later, following a large assembly of unemployed workers at Parliament, Kirkcaldie & Stains lost 11 of the 24 large windows that fronted on to Lambton Quay. The DIC next door lost four of its 18 windows. The tantalising consumer goods on display behind expensive, imported plate-glass windows represented the unequal distribution of resources apparent in a society almost at the point of melt-down; yet there was virtually no looting reported from department stores. The act of breaking through each of those transparent yet powerful barriers seems to have been symbolic and sufficient.

Although two of the distinguishing characteristics of department stores were that there was never any compulsion to buy and free access was offered to all, by the 1930s many of these erstwhile drapery stores, now grown far beyond their founders' imaginings, were perceived as comfortably middle-class institutions, at the heart of an increasingly urbanised New Zealand society. Each city had a pecking order. 'There was a hierarchy of Christchurch department stores with Ballantyne's at the top and Armstrong's and Miller's for working people', stated one historian of the city's workers and their work places.[33] In Auckland each store had its own rank.[34] One elderly shopper firmly recollected 'I wouldn't have gone to John Court's — no — but Milne & Choyce and Smith & Caughey — yes'.[35] Auckland Grammar School teacher Frank Rogers had accounts with Milne & Choyce, which he saw as progressive and adventurous, catering for the rising middle class, as well as with the more conservative Smith & Caughey's; he remembered often shopping at John Court with its more popular style and occasionally at George Court's and Farmers'.[36] Farmers' in Auckland clearly did not target an upper-middle-class clientele. A graphic designer in the advertising department of Farmers', awarded second prize in a 1940s staff essay competition on 'The Future of Farmers'', was called to the general manager's office. The designer had suggested that there should be a broadening of Farmers' target market and an increased interest in higher-class and better-quality goods, 'What about "Mrs Remuera"?' the young man challenged. W. Calder Mackay, the general manager, looked westward through his office window, gestured towards the then working-class suburbs of Grey Lynn and Ponsonby and replied 'this is the market we are aiming at; we are not interested in "Mrs Remuera"'.[37]

Customers from a range of classes, however, shopped in all of these stores and appreciated the services they offered. Despite one journalist writing in 1980 that 'Queen Street has always looked to Karangahape Road with some disdain, never quite saying it in so many words, but nevertheless making it clear that K-Road was no more than its working class cousin, barely tolerated', the perception did not necessarily reflect people's shopping practices.

Farmers' always identified with the working-class man, his wife and family though as business prospered, its range of customers had broadened. It was in step with 'the worker's friend', Miller's of Christchurch, which survived the Great Depression by selling well-made clothing at low prices.[38] Gum-diggers would send their monthly orders to Farmers' in advance, to be filled as soon as their tally of gum had been assessed and paid for. Sometimes there was insufficient money from the sale to meet the cost of their order and non-essential items would have to be weeded out of the list by Farmers' staff. In the early 1930s, young Rawdon Busfield, a Baptist Church member, later to hold an important managerial role in Farmers', decided that tobacco was one of those dispensable commodities. It was definitely not a judgment that was

'From factory to farm': Farmers' Catalogue No.7, published in the mid-1920s.
126285½, ALEXANDER TURNBULL LIBRARY, WELLINGTON.

appreciated by the Northland gum-diggers. As the store's name indicated, a significant number of Farmers' customers were workers in the rural scene, and the firm's guarantee of 'Satisfaction or Money Back' particularly appealed, especially to those buying sight unseen. Like George Blackwell's 'Railway Store', which was set up in Kaiapoi in 1871, Farmers' recognised the rural as well as the urban consumer's needs. Blackwell's stocked groceries and operated a cart and harness section as well as drapery and clothing, with regular country rounds serving surrounding districts with the creak of wheels and the crack of whip. When the railway eventually reached Kaiapoi, the commercial centre of the town moved, and astute Blackwell, like many of his counterparts in larger cities, shifted his business. Expansion into Weston's larger store on the corner of Hilton and Black Streets in 1873 allowed Blackwell's the addition of a bakery, a produce store and a stable.[39]

George Blackwell's store in Kaiapoi. 011094, ALEXANDER TURNBULL LIBRARY, WELLINGTON.

Smith & Caughey's had early established a flourishing national mail-order business, publishing regular catalogues and advertising in newspapers and periodicals, including the Maori language *Te Korimako*.[40] Publications sent to rural customers included lavishly illustrated guidebooks showing the latest styles for women. The *Silent Traveller and Fashion Guide* was the discreet title of Kirkcaldie & Stains' 1899 seasonal mail-order catalogue.[41] Ballantynes continually advertised widely in periodicals as diverse as the *Mirror* and the *Methodist Times*. Such stores, and there were a number throughout New Zealand with large mail-order departments, had to contend with the scale and extent of Farmers' operations, but were frequently targeting a more up-market clientele. A reflection on its distinctive development, by 1929 Robert Laidlaw was proudly boasting that Farmers' had 'the largest mail order business in the Dominion'.[42] Farmers' catalogues offered an extraordinarily diverse selection of 'drapery, clothing, hardware, furniture, footwear, crockery, stationery, jewellery, saddlery, harness, farm implements, grocery and produce'. Suspended by string, the pages from out-of-date catalogues were reportedly put to a very practical end use in many thrifty households.[43] Often accompanying the bulky and fascinating inventories in the mail-out were smaller, supplementary advertising and promotional leaflets. If no response was received from the recipient of a Farmers' catalogue, encouraging follow-up letters would be sent, tracked through a well-organised records system.[44] Mail-order acumen and a sharp sense of timing was revealed when, just over one month after the earthquake of 3 February 1931, a Farmers' advertisement appeared in the local Napier paper offering a thirty-two-piece dinner set, worth £3, for 2s 6d, with any bedroom, lounge or dining-room suite over £16. The suite and dinner set would be packed free and delivered to Auckland station or wharf on receipt of 2s 6d. Payment could be made by small weekly instalments.[45]

Ordering by mail was well and good, but rural customers headed straight for the stores when they were in town. It was the experience of actually being there, in those grand, bustling stores, that set them apart from run-of-the-mill shopping and made them such an enduring presence in New Zealanders' memories. House & Daking of Hamilton welcomed 'Visitors to the Waikato Winter Show [who] are invited to make Free Use of the Lounge, Rest Rooms, Telephone and other facilities provided for their use, without charge or obligation.'[46] Young Bob Harvey would have been familiar with Farmers' and its bargains, but George Court's, close to home, was nevertheless 'the best'. With its spectacular window-runs, lofty ceilings and a staircase noted by one architect as being the finest of its time in the Auckland area, it presented an image of bourgeois grandeur that was missing from Farmers' more utilitarian, ex-warehouse building. Entering with a stream of customers through one of the several street doors, past the wooden, glass-fronted counters with their stacks of multi-coloured gloves and handbags, socks and ties, beyond the beautiful young female assistants at the cosmetic counters, wafting a hint of perfume, and the smart floor-walker, a natty dresser in dapper morning suit, Bob and other customers made their way into the busy ground floor.

The street-level floor was viewed as the most important of all the floors and its arrangement was paramount. New Zealand department-store management took heed of the wisdom of their overseas counterparts as they planned for the future. When pre-World War I plans for the new DIC building in Dunedin were reviewed in post-war times, it was arranged that George Crow (the store's manager) would visit the United States and Great Britain to make sure that the interior was up to date in style and function.[47] During the Depression, H. & J. Smith's Invercargill store was completely re-designed by an Australian expert, T. J. Clark.[48] As well as visits to Britain, Europe and America for buying purposes, an increasing volume of trade literature kept management staff and buyers in New Zealand informed about trends in the United States and Britain. Each floor of the stores was allocated according to a 'traditionally' prescribed and successful pattern. Even if extra height and floors were added to buildings in order to maximise increasing land value, those additions did not markedly change the ground floor layout. Vertical expansion was firmly based on the secure foundation of a busy ground floor. The lively and vibrant ground floor offered an exciting, central focus for the world of consumption. Each season the traditional patrons of department stores discovered the 'new' yet again, using a well established template to navigate modernity.

With its great diversity of goods, many arranged in small, yet separate departments, the ground floor could be seen as the department store in microcosm. Departmentalisation enabled customers' needs to be readily served, while ensuring that management could keep a watchful eye over the financial performance of each section in relation to the whole store.

The central cash-desk, the pulsing heart of the store's financial operations, with lively links to each selling counter, was usually located on the ground floor. Staffed by extra cashiers at sale times, this busy space was served by a circulation system of

John Court's ground floor, c.1950. Rows of fluorescent tubes have replaced incandescent lighting. The Lamson tubes are clearly visible winding their way up columns and along the ceiling.
PHOTOGRAPH: WALTER J. THOMPSON. REAY CLARKE COLLECTION, J. GRANT.

metal tubes, winding their way through walls and along ceilings, and powered by a substantial electric turbine in the basement. The Lamson pneumatic tube system represented pervasive modernity as it swallowed up dockets and money encased in metal 'carriers', and coughed up the requisite change in a return capsule. If turn-around took an inordinately long time, impatient sales assistants would sometimes deliver a few sharp raps on the metal cover of the tube's opening, which usually seemed to have the required effect on the cashier. If a customer had a charge account, confirmation was needed that the balance was healthy enough for the sale to proceed and the goods

Lamson tube capsules from George Court's. The money raised by the sale of the metal tubing when it was finally removed from George Court's building was sufficient to pay for the replacement cash registers. G. FORTUNE.

to leave the store. Shop assistants developed the subtle art of 'slow wrapping' so that if necessary, the credit manager had time to appear and conduct the necessary interview with a customer whose payments might be falling behind.[49]

Despite mice, and other foreign bodies being placed in the carriers, the occasional blockages of the tubes, or a broken turbine blade, 'when the noise was deafening and could be heard all over the store', the system was reliable and efficient.[50] A 'Lamson Shute' was installed when Kirkcaldie & Stains' new building was constructed in 1908 and operated until the store was renovated in the 1980s.[51] For Ballantynes, the newer

Lamson pneumatic system replaced an earlier, gravity-driven, 'Lamson Cash Railway' installed in 1892, which used overhead wires to convey payment and receipts. Although Ballantynes' brass Lamson tubes did not survive the 1947 fire, a similar system of steel tubes replaced them in the new building, and was retained until the 1990s.[52] Smith & Caughey's, H. & J. Smith's, Arthur Barnett's, and Penrose's Lamson systems, together with many others around New Zealand, all gave decades of sterling service.[53]

Apart from those vital cash operations, there was a general agreement on the layout of selling floors by the end of the first decade of the twentieth century. The street level or ground floor was to offer 'cosmetics, notions, gloves, hosiery, jewelry and other small wares — glamour and impulse items to waylay women on their way to the upper floors — and clothing and furnishings for men who were presumed too timid to venture further into the store'.[54] It was not only men who might be shy. Janet Frame recalled a brave foray into a Dunedin department store:

> I daringly went to the cosmetic counter at the D.I.C., where the assistant testing lip-
> sticks on the back of my hand chose 'my' shade of 'Tangee'. I bought rose milk for
> my skin and Evening in Paris perfume in its deep blue bottle. And seeing my efforts to
> 'make something of myself', as they expressed it, the other waitresses were pleased.
> 'Now you're one of us,' they said.[55]

Not only did the ground floor display a profusion of smaller affordable items, its design also encouraged easy progression through the aisles to the electric lifts, which were usually situated well towards the rear of the building. Elevators had been considered marvels of technology when installed in department stores, literally symbolising the heights of modernity. A lift had been installed in Ballantynes' Timaru store in 1913. When the store was rebuilt in 1986, the lift cage and its associated mechanisms, a working example of historic machinery, were consigned to a local museum.[56] Lifts were designed to shift large numbers of people quickly and effortlessly, and were operated by smartly uniformed and gloved attendants who functioned with expertise, power and authority. At busy times, they regulated the number of people allowed 'on board' and relegated others to waiting queues. For youngsters like Bob, the intoned litany of departments as the lifts soared heavenward was interwoven with mysterious, unknown terms that were acquired as part of the department store experience. The significance of 'manchester' and 'mercery', 'hosiery' and

McGruer's department store in New Plymouth filled their display windows with an assortment
of appealing haberdashery and goods. 015403, ALEXANDER TURNBULL LIBRARY, WELLINGTON.

'haberdashery', 'mantles' and 'millinery', 'napery' and 'lingerie' all needed to be learned and understood in order to negotiate the floors with confidence.

The throng of 1920s department store customers was dressed in suitably formal attire, whether for work or for a day's shopping, with the requisite hats, gloves and 'best outfits' for women, matched by hats, ties and suits for men. Children like Bob modelled the fashions of their elders.[57] Shopping in town was an occasion in itself. Suitably clad, the public ventured into the ground floors of their regular department stores, prepared either 'to buy or not to buy', for that was indeed the question which would ensure the stores' viability. Like other department-store employees, female shop assistants in Smith & Caughey's matched the mode with equivalent formality. They were 'expected to wear black or a uniform of approved style and colour. Male assistants are expected to wear black or dark grey coats, and not to be without coats if possible after 11 a.m., or whenever attending to customers.'[58] Ballantynes' female shop assistants wore black dresses with white collars and no jewellery was tolerated. Men wore dark suits and white collars.[59] John Court's 1920 staff rule book allowed its female assistants to wear white blouses in summer, but, to curb any wild sartorial excesses, directed that 'men must wear dark clothes and starched collars, and avoid unusual colour combinations of hosiery and neckwear'.[60] Through the 1920s, Kirkcaldie & Stains' female staff still wore their formal black.[61] An *Auckland Star* photograph from the hot January days of 1929 recorded a daring exception with the caption: 'Suitable attire for hot weather — employees of Rendells Ltd have set an example for cool summer working dress. They are wearing shirts of the lumber-jacket pattern.'[62] Several young men, looking slightly ill at ease, wearing ties and long-sleeved white shirts of a rather odd design, gathered to the waist, stood in line for the photographer. The fashion did not catch on with other department store staff.

As well as the smart service and window displays, the special items on show, together with regular advertising, all contributed to the allure of the department stores. These factors helped entice even the most hesitant customers into store precincts, and succeeded in delivering them to the furthest reaches of these communities of consumption. Here the full measure of 'consumer democracy' could be exercised. This concept was conveyed most markedly on the ground floor, with modern methods in presentation used to promote its wares to prospective consumers and to those who, like young Bob, might be 'just looking'. Paul Nystrom's sequence of maxims for selling — 'arrested attention, the arousal of interest, inspection leading to desire and finally, purchase' were key components for the success of the street-level floor.[63]

Department stores are usually considered female spaces, and much of their written history is imbued with the trope of seduction and with images of female desire; so the time-honoured allocation of ground floor space to men as consumers is of particular interest.[64] Clothes can be added to 'house and car' as signifiers of status, occupation and identity for men.[65] New Zealand department stores, those important indicators of modern style and fashion for women, were among the major providers of clothing for men of all ages, who were consumers in their own right, as well as economic providers for their wives and families.

Although there have been several international studies on men and their roles in the culture of consumption, society, and the world of fashion, little has been written on the subject in New Zealand. Works have focused on the relationship between fashion and masculinity, and on advertising and the male body, while yet another explored the ways in which white-collar manliness became a signifier of masculinity in the 1950s.[66] Danielle Sprecher challenged the view that men were not interested in male fashion and argued that the masculine consumer did indeed exist in the so-called 'Adamless Eden' of the inter-war New Zealand department store.[67]

Although Sprecher stated that during this period department stores developed 'what they called "men's shops" within the store . . . designed to cater to the male consumer and . . . therefore constructed as especially masculine spaces', New Zealand as well as overseas department stores had already evolved their ground floors to reflect what were the accepted, gendered patterns of usage.[68] As Leach noted, in the United States:

> those conditions would go unchanged even as department stores opened their doors to men in a big way in the early 1920s. Over time men had separate street and elevator entrances and separate departments, or 'stores,' dressed in dark and rugged colours. Everything was done to create distinct gender spaces for men and women, even as (or especially because) the exigencies of the capitalist market pulled them more closely together than ever before in the public domain. The motive was not to prevent sexual interaction in public (which might have been the case in another culture) but to give men psychological peace of mind.[69]

The allocation of space for male consumers had been established in New Zealand's stores well before the 1920s. An 1860s sketch of Kirkcaldie & Stains' first shop 'on the beach' in Wellington showed a bold advertisement for 'Mens [sic] Hosiers and Linen

Drapers' painted directly on the building. An 1872 advertisement for new stock at Dunstable House in Christchurch, at the time John Ballantyne acquired the business, included men's, boys' and youths' clothing.[70] At the opening of new extensions to Milne & Choyce's leased premises on the corner of Wellesley Street East and Queen Street in 1900, it was announced that 'for 26 years they have given their undivided attention to the ladies, and for men this house has been a forbidden place. They have, however, now decided to devote this new portion of their premises which will be 60ft. by 20ft. wide, to gentlemen's mercery, boys' clothing, etc.'[71] By the early 1900s, Ballantynes had separate departments for 'men's clothing and mercery' on their ground floor.[72] Smith & Caughey's early advertised 'Gent's Mercery and Clothing Departments' in their Auckland store.[73] Although their menswear department was always sited on the ground floor of the store, by December 1916 they were also offering a third-floor 'Waiting Room for men, where they may refresh themselves by a wash and brush-up after the heat and dust of the city'.[74] This kept pace with John Court, which had just opened a sixth-floor gentlemen's smoking lounge, complete with furniture 'in two shades of dark brown'.[75]

At the end of the 1930s John Court's 'Men's Shop', with its own street entrance and adjacent department for youths and boys, was well established on the ground floor, together with 'handbags, hosiery, handkerchiefs, gloves, umbrellas, toiletries and cosmetics, wools, haberdashery, needleworkers' needs and stationery'.[76] This department had been opened in 1933 — 'until recently the department for Boys' and Children's wearables' — and in the 'friendly seclusion of this modern Men's Shop, (adjoining JCL's Main Store, and entered directly from Queen Street) . . . a man can give expression, full and untrammeled, to discrimination and taste'.[77] George Court's menswear section on the ground floor also had a separate entrance, with men's and boys' footwear departments situated on the third floor.[78] This store also incorporated a men's smoking room, on the fourth floor adjacent to the tearoom.[79] Milne & Choyce's newly extended building, situated 'between the banks' in Queen Street, had incorporated a men's mercery department on the ground floor with men's clothing and tailoring departments on the first floor, which was known as the 'Men's Floor'. Here 'on your own Floor, a modernly appointed Barber's shop (with six chairs), offering a quick and efficient service. Whatever particular style you wish in hairdressing is followed meticulously and that well-groomed look achieved with the utmost satisfaction.'[80] From the 1920s through the 1950s, the fashion of a 'short back and sides' hair-style for

What the well-dressed man might be wearing around Wellington in the 1940s. Stylish felt hats for men in James Smith's store window. PA COLLECTION 3332 – 03 29, ALEXANDER TURNBULL LIBRARY, WELLINGTON.

men required frequent and regular trimming. The barber's shop provided an incentive for the great number of professional and businessmen working in the city to visit the first floor regularly.[81] Kirkcaldie & Stains, too, had a 'Men's Toilet Salon' where a shave or a haircut would be among the services on offer.[82]

Menswear departments were spaces where men were encouraged to feel comfortable and secluded. In order to achieve this separation within the ground floor, several were long and narrow in proportion, often stretching the depth of the store and not necessarily close to the elevators. Australian historian Gail Reekie maintains that 'by the 1930s, it was an accepted "psychological fact" that men had an aversion to walking through women's departments'.[83] At the end of 1929, James Smith's in Wellington advertised:

> Our Men's Annexe on the east side of the building, served by a special entrance on
> the Manners St frontage, houses the finest Men's and Boys' Clothing Departments
> to be found anywhere in the Dominion. Here men can, although in a Department
> Store, enter, secure their wants, and leave without in any way making contact with the
> General Drapery Departments. You will be amazed at the extent and scope of the fine
> Men's Sections housed in the Annexe. A store within a store, splendidly planned for
> men and entirely staffed by men and served by a distinct and separate entrance.[84]

Not only could men avoid passing through any other space than that allocated to their needs, but women, too, if they so desired, could steer well clear of a department which dealt exclusively with outfitting the male body.

The view of men as shy and uncertain shoppers, needing the reassurance of an environment tailored to their needs, was not always sustained by contemporary writing in retail trade literature, which portrayed the typical male as more purposeful than hesitant. Having decided what he wished to buy, he entered, purchased, and exited the store as quickly as possible.[85] Sometimes these forays could be surprisingly adventurous, and nothing to do with fashion. Armstrong's of Christchurch offered 'Whitebaiters! The whitebait season starts early. Be sure and get your share of Armstrong's famous Mosquito Net.'[86] George Court's proffered several patterns of male consumerism in one 1932 advertisement, but the predominant assumption was that men shopped for themselves: 'Men who buy their shirts hastily without much thought — or men who shop carefully and know value when they find it — or even men who don't shop at all but let their wives do it — all will be delighted with this shirt . . . not cheap shirts but good shirts at a low price'.[87]

In the years when shirts had detachable collars, secured by studs at front and back neckline, James Smith's enticed men to join its 'Famous Collar Club. Free Collars for Life. Life membership 10/- including 1 dozen new collars.'[88] A decade later, the fashion for separate collars was on the wane. George Court's were advertising the latest 'Coat shirts, Sports shirt and Negligé shirts'. The coat shirts and sports shirts had their collars firmly attached, while the charmingly named 'negligé shirts' still had separate collars.[89]

Department stores adopted up-to-date advertising strategies to encourage men as well as women into their shops. American advertising agencies had grown enormously during the inter-war period and New Zealand firms eagerly incorporated their ideas. To god-fearing Dunedin in 1925, Brown, Ewing addressed a somewhat flippant advertisement: 'Alas! — the end is Near — Yes its' [sic] sad but true! Brown, Ewing's Annual Summer Sale positively closes on Saturday next, February 14th. The End is Very Near.'[90] Appealing to the younger male, a 1934 advertisement for a Battersby hat costing 16s 6d was accompanied by a pin-up style photograph of a handsome man, his broad-brimmed felt hat on a dashing angle. John Court suggested that 'young men will instantly recognise "The Big Shot" as the type of Hat which they have seen worn so effectively on the screen by their favourite film stars . . . . This is the hat that has gone to the heads of England's smartest men — Be among the first to wear it in Auckland.'[91] Using stylish illustrations in their advertisements, which changed from day to day, department stores employed talented staff who consistently targeted young, middle-aged and older men with smart, modern and streetwise copy. In newspapers and journals, they portrayed themselves as appealing to modern male consumers, using advertisements for men's clothing that emphasised achievement and social standing, and almost invariably depicted a tall, handsome, dignified and clearly successful man of indeterminate age — the modern gentleman. If, as a young man, one aspired to be a member of the professional or business community of town or city, or if one had already reached those ranks, department stores were the places to buy the clothes appropriate for such status. 'Gentlemen appreciate good taste and refinement in personal appearance first', stated an advertisement for men's suits by Blythe's of Napier.[92]

It went without saying that such gentlemen would be well educated. Ballantynes used a deliberate misquote from Shakespeare's *Hamlet* to convey their message: '"The apparel doth oft betray the man." We can't evade the fact that the clothes we wear react upon the mind. An ill-chosen suit may depress. One well-chosen will exhilarate. Ballantynes offer exceptional choice of highest-grade Hand Craft Suits, hand tailored throughout from 10 guineas.'[93] George Court's copywriter also targeted middle-class male consumers with literary leanings, quoting novelist Arnold Bennett: '"fashion is neither absurd nor negligible; it is one of the most powerful influences upon human conduct — an influence which nobody can escape"'. The advertisement continued: 'Much has been written on the importance of a smart appearance, but Arnold Bennett covers the whole subject in the above few words. How far the "Influence" of smart apparel can lead is impossible to say . . . in business, in pleasure, in every sphere of life its importance is noticed. Are YOUR clothes a credit to YOU?'[94] In attributing literary knowledge as well as thoughtful consideration to their targets, such advertising deliberately credited men with rationality and intelligence in their choice of clothing. The male shopper was identified with reason.[95] 'It's good business to dress well . . . . You'll realize it when you look about at the successful business men you know. Smartly cut, well-fitting clothes are a sound investment in self assurance . . . and to achieve such clothing without paying any more than you need, consult George Court's Men's Shop.'[96] In such advertising, the potential customer 'was cast as a variant of economic man, calculating and in control'.[97]

In 1933, at a time of grave economic conditions, the September issue of the *Auckland Chamber of Commerce Journal*, with a predominantly male circulation, was published as a 'Business Men's Apparel Number'. It featured Smith & Caughey's stylish new Lippincott building on the cover as one of the leading Auckland department stores. The main feature, entitled 'Are Men Becoming More Clothes-Conscious? — A Symposium', featured articles on the latest in spring fashion for men, contributed by J. R. Rendell, J. T. McCorkindale (a buyer at Milne & Choyce's men's department), R. K. Angus of George Court's, C. W. H. Cox from John Court, and Hugh Wright. Except for the latter, all were representatives of major department stores in the city. Editorial comment reinforced their authority by stating that 'it has been said that New Zealand men generally are badly dressed. Auckland sartorial experts refute this accusation, and indicate the new styles which we shall all be wearing before long.'[98] The whole apparel issue endeavoured to improve interest in men's clothing. It carried advertisements for John Court's re-vamped menswear department. Court's offered 'spring suits tailored to your individual measurement, from 95 / - [£4 15s]'.[99] Although neither Smith & Caughey's nor Farmers' menswear buyers were among those contributing articles to that issue, all the department stores were listed as members of the Auckland Chamber of Commerce; towards the back was the usual advertisement for Farmers': 'The Dominion's Largest Department Store'.[100]

In the 1930s department stores saw themselves as leaders in the vanguard of masculine style. They promoted the fashion sense of the younger man, epitomised by Edward, Prince of Wales, 'who has ever been ready to give a lead in innovation without ostentation'. Masculine style was equated with English style, which, together with the latest fashion colour of 'Cambridge green', was the focus of the Auckland Chamber of Commerce symposium. Hugh Wright stated with some prescience that 'the younger men perhaps are more appreciative of dress than their elders and perhaps the next generation will develop a style suitable to our New Zealand life. I refer particularly to the New Zealander's love of sports suits and flannels — a style of dress in which to my mind they definitely outclass the average Englishman.'[101] In Christchurch, traditional styles continued to appeal. Just a year earlier Armstrong's had advertised new season's men's straw boaters 'just arrived from England'.[102] Ballantynes announced 'the Return of the Straw Boater. In Men's attire there are not many opportunities for an entire change; for this reason the reintroduction of the Straw Boater has been heartily welcomed as correct style for Spring and Summer wear.'[103]

Although no longer worn with straw boaters, which usually kept company with blazers and flannels, suits were required in all seasons for day, casual, and evening wear. They had become an international symbol of respectable masculinity, an 'unofficial uniform of power', with New Zealand males conforming to this principle.[104] Tailored suits were the definitive clothing for a professional or businessman and, by implication, the ultimate model of aspiring masculinity for many New Zealanders. A significant number of men chose department stores to tailor those suits. Brown, Ewing of Dunedin were confidently advertising 'Suits that make admiring friends ask "Who's your tailor?" . . . Meet our Mr Easton — ! An Expert Tailor of long experience.'[105] Albert Feslier had been at the head of the men's tailoring department at Kirkcaldie & Stains from the early 1920s. 'According to one distinguished customer [he was] "the best tailor in the world"; the only problem with his suits was that they never wore out.'[106] In offering these services the stores were in competition with specialty tailors, one of whom somewhat subversively offered an alternative to the straight 'reason why' advertising of the large stores. Shortly after the Queen Street riots, Peter Mack the master tailor advertised from the relative safety of the Strand Arcade: 'Just look

From blazers and flannels to the latest in tailored suits complete with
double–breasted waistcoats, a range of men's fashion is modelled in the 1930s.
PHOTOGRAPH: F. E. MCGREGOR. 1982.122.8, CANTERBURY MUSEUM.

at our window! There's more than a few breakages to hold your interest here. Come and feast your eyes on the display of our new suitings waiting to be made up into your "Petermack" — tailored to your measurements for a fiver! Come in this week (N.B., through the door, please).'[107]

In 1920 Blythe's of Napier had been offering made-to-measure suits at £8 17s 6d.[108] Ever mindful of its remote country customers, in 1923 Farmers' Trading Company sent a mail-order leaflet offering a made-to-measure suit at £3 15s, with a do-it-yourself measuring chart and tape, together with free fabric samples.[109] A 1927 catalogue from Farmers' advertised navy serge made-to-measure suits for £5 17s 6d, urging that 'no matter how many Tweed Suits you may have, a Blue Serge will be a worthwhile addition. Greys and Browns, Woollens and Worsteds, Herringbones and Twills may come and go in fashion, but a genuine Navy Blue Serge Suit is always in good taste, and is the dressiest of all suits.'[110] During the Depression, when prices fell, department stores could still offer their tailor-made suits at better rates than bespoke tailors, because of the quantity sold.[111] They could negotiate good prices for bulk orders of tweed, wool and worsted, the quality of fabric being of equal if not more importance than cut and style. Ballantynes with its first-floor tailoring department stated with authority: 'When buying a suit, the primary consideration is the selection of the cloth . . . . The second essential is the construction of the suit.'[112]

In 1934, Milne & Choyce proudly reported that they had obtained the services of a first-class English cutter from London, at ten guineas per week, for their high-class tailoring business.[113] A 1935 advertisement from the *Auckland Star* deployed an image of power and organisation, advising men to make George Court's their 'headquarters'.[114] This firm was promoting made-to-measure men's suits at a cost of £3 17s 6d, including three expert fittings. 'George Court's famous all-the-year-round offer permits no reduction whatever — not even during sale period.'[115] By August, over 1200 of those 'quality suits' had been sold that year.[116]

In mid-December 1925, the DIC in Wellington offered to take orders for 'your holiday suit' made to measure for delivery before Christmas. This was no relaxed holiday, spent on beach or lake-shore in casual clothes, for a smartly attired, suited gentleman, complete with hat, tie, waistcoat and cane illustrated the advertisement.[117] Vacations allowed no dropping of sartorial standards.

A single suit was clearly not enough. Milne & Choyce encouraged men to 'dress for the occasion' with smart outfits for formal and casual wear, as well as plus-fours and argyle socks for golf. The pressure was on men to be consumers in high style. 'The well dressed man should have at least four suits and have shoes, shirts, hats, ties, sox etc to go with each. This may sound extravagant perhaps, but if one wears a suit for two weeks and then changes, each suit would only get thirteen week's [*sic*] wear in a year, so work out how good looking your suits and all accessories would be three years after your first outlay', brightly suggested Milne & Choyce's menswear buyer, with little admission that changing fashions might render all one's suits out of date.[118]

In 1940, after the outbreak of World War II, the price of George Court's made-to-measure suits increased to £5 19s 6d, with out-of-town customers able to write for free patterns and a self-measuring form. That master of tailoring Albert Feslier had retired from Kirkcaldie & Stains in the late 1930s, and died in 1943.[119] In early 1944, after the death of Mr Evans of the men's tailoring department at Milne & Choyce, it was decided to close the department because of the difficulty of obtaining skilled labour during the war.[120] With that closure, a foreshadowing of the passage of the made-to-measure suit as the ultimate men's fashion statement, might also have been observed.

If a made-to-measure suit was out of the question, a ready-made suit 'off the peg' was the alternative. Each department store had its own range, with workrooms producing in-house brands. In December 1929, when Hay's of Christchurch opened its doors for the first time, one of the two full-page advertisements for the new store was wholly given over to men, offering them a 'Maclone suit — a low priced quality' garment sold exclusively by Hay's.[121] In that same month, James Smith's of Wellington advertised 'John Sincerity' suits, each one delivered properly packed in 'a special Christmas Box' — a small suitcase, 12 inches long and 18 inches wide.[122] By 1934, Smith & Caughey's were advertising men's superior quality, navy serge suits, recommended for lasting service and smart appearance. This famous 'Imperial' make was reduced to £4 3s 6d, £4 14s 6d and £5 1s at the July sales, and men's two-piece tweed suits in good-wearing brown and fawn tweeds were reduced to £2 9s 6d.[123]

As the war effort began to take over the country's efforts and resources, khaki, air-force blue and navy blue replaced alternative colours of woollen fabric on the production line as clothing factories turned to making uniforms rather than civilian clothes. Newspaper advertisements for department stores became fewer and smaller. Ballantynes advertised less frequently, often only once a fortnight.[124] Even the newspapers themselves were reduced in size.

Rationing of petrol, food, clothing, footwear and household linen was imposed in 1942 in order to reduce New Zealanders' consumption of these items by one third. Each person had an allocation of 52 clothing units or coupons for each twelve-month period. A man's three-piece suit required sixteen coupons, an overcoat twelve coupons, and a raincoat eight.[125] When servicemen were returning to New Zealand, 'strong unbleached overalls for painters, dairy workers, mechanics etc' were offered for two coupons each, as were 'new sports trousers'.[126] Women's shoes took two coupons, but men's shoes required three.[127] All footwear was in short supply, and Ballantynes' plan to open a shoe department was delayed until 1945 because of a lack of stock.[128] George Court's offered the opportunity to have existing shoes 'rebuilt', a process that promised 'more than just repairing'.[129]

By the early 1950s, however, after this period of enforced limitations, department stores were again urging men to buy clothes, including suits and accessories, but generally in a more relaxed and informal way. In 1951 an advertisement offered 'Winter Weight Pyjamas — but don't wait for the winter. Just wait till she sees you in a pair of George Court's Viyella Pyjamas . . . you can't? Well then come right in now and see them yourself.'[130] In 1952 it was suggested that men should consider buying 'Pugaree Hat Bands' as part of their holiday wardrobes. These were 'separate adjustable hat bands in all the colours needed to match different suit shades — only 6/- each'.[131] Instead of conforming to such genteel aphorisms as 'ostentation is the worst form of vulgarity', it was suggested that men's clothes be promoted 'with much more "sizzle" to catch the imagination of the customer'.[132] Men had been discovering the undercover daring of 'Summer Sensation Jungle Jockey shorts — the famous Jungle Prints — 10/6 a pair' at department stores and men's specialty stores.[133] Men's clothes were increasingly casual as forecast by Hugh Wright in the 1930s, with much less emphasis on made-to-measure outfits. Formerly, men had been apologetic about wearing ready-made suits; that was changing, and the '"off the peg" suit has become respectable, aided by immense advertising efforts'.[134] A modern outlook was now expressed by choosing an off-the-rack suit in the latest in colour, fabric, and style. By 1959, the DIC in Wellington was promoting 'American tropical weight dacron' suits as being 'ideal for business and casual wear. Lightweight cool and crease resisting, they pack into a surprisingly small space for travelling.'[135] Increasingly, air travel, both within and beyond New Zealand was becoming a significant indicator of modernity.

Expenditure on 'apparel and personal accessories' grew only slowly between 1954 and 1964.[136] 'In the mid 1950's', stated one economist, 'the average New Zealander considered himself well fed and adequately clothed. This may be presumed because in the following decade he did not increase his expenditure on food and clothing by very much, even though his income increased substantially. Rather, he spent more on consumer durables (refrigerators, radios, washing machines, television sets, motor cars and telephones), on commodities associated with the durables (electricity and petrol), and on certain leisure activities such as internal and overseas travel.'[137] In September 1955, when an exciting Italian collection of women's clothing was being paraded at Kirkcaldie & Stains in Wellington, across the road at the neighbouring DIC the equivalent highlight for men was a daily 'demonstration by Mr K. Higgins in the Hardware Section' of the 'KBC "Powerchief" in action!' as it 'saws. drills. polishes: Grooves and rebates: Grinds and buffs: Sands and polishes: complete standard kitset at the fabulously low price of £18.2.0 cash'.[138] Through the 1950s, with the establishment of many new homes in spreading suburbs, expenditure on major items such as cars, together with tools and household appliances, became greater than ever before. The number of registered motor vehicles in New Zealand more than doubled from 210,027 in 1947 to 515,173 in 1960.[139] Petrol rationing had gone, and increasingly men were using cars to travel to work at a distance from their homes, not necessarily in the heart of cities and towns.

How did this affect department stores? Social and cultural historians studying the development of masculinity and the phenomenon of the 1980s 'New Man' have agreed that the 1950s and the 1960s were critical decades in which a new youth culture, prosperity, and the explosion of post-war consumerism undermined the concept of formal dress, and relegated such clothing to the middle-class, middle-aged and conservative.[140] 'From the 1930s to the mid-1950s, selling techniques [in the menswear market had] relied on one clearly identifiable icon. This was the image of the gentleman.'[141] Despite efforts to project more casual informality, department stores found it difficult to shed this restrictive gender image; as a traditional model of masculinity it had always been an important component of their advertising discourse. When Hallenstein's marked their one hundred and tenth anniversary in 1984, the author of their celebratory booklet wrote that 'the "consensus" society of the 1940's and 1950's, with its fixed social standards and conformity of fashion in male apparel, has quietly been forgotten'.[142]

Menswear stores such as Keene's in Auckland, with its iconic, cowboy neon sign, were already advertising American jeans in the late 1950s, while Levi Strauss were to commandeer the youth market in the 1960s.[143] Young men were becoming important consumers in their own right and they were increasingly conforming to their own new fashions of the off-beat, the outrageous and the uncommon — ranges of clothing which could not be economically stocked by department stores, even if they had wished to do so. The worry about 'unusual colour combinations of hosiery and neckwear', which had so concerned John Court's 1920s staff management, seemed ludicrous by 1960. 'Men go as gay as their families on the beaches this summer. And in the male world the latest high fashion bracket of casual clothes must include shirts and shorts in different colour combinations on a black background' wrote a keen copywriter in 1958.[144] It was a far cry from 'What-To-Wear A Surfing This Summer' in 1935, where 'Men's all-wool Roslyn "Hippies"' with white belts featured, as well as men's full bathing costumes with a full or half skirt and a 'racer back'. The Jantzen 'Two-Some' offered a discreet maroon or black 'complete' bathing suit 'convertible into a pair of smart Trunks by simply releasing the zip fastening at waist'.[145] The growing variety of men's clothing, including the burgeoning youth market, could no longer be catered for, let alone contained, within the traditionally gendered and isolated space allocated to menswear on the ground floor.

By the 1950s, modern escalators, new symbols of modernity on the move, were being installed, transporting people up from the ground floor through the stores. They supplemented the faithful lifts and provided a novel experience for customers of all ages.[146] Whereas the DIC's 1929 escalator in Wellington had been the first in New Zealand, and Miller's in Christchurch had installed the first escalator in the South Island ten years later, it was not until December 1954 that Farmers' unveiled the first in Auckland. Together with other local dignitaries, a rather disgruntled and bad-tempered Hector, the store's famous parrot, was carried up from floor to floor, with due ceremony to mark the occasion.[147] His displeasure might have sounded a warning, for the next day a customer who had been generously offered the opportunity to be the first to use this new and convenient way to reach the heights of the building, fell over at the top of the first section; she had to be taken to the nurse's room for first-aid attention.

Department stores were having more and more difficulty enticing potential customers up from the ground floor; if this could not be accomplished it was a risk to the whole operation. 'To lift oneself from the hustle and bustle of everyday life into a cloud of make-believe is the only escape our minds can do with ease; and the colourful imagination that oft-times runs riot can be gently eased back to reality simply by visiting a frock salon, [or by] the purchase of a fashionable tie.'[148] The ground floors of department stores could always be relied upon to offer a good selection of men's ties, but men were beginning to abandon ties and cravats in favour of more informality.

For young children like Bob Harvey, though, long before any interest in ties might develop, a voyage of discovery to the interesting things available upstairs in the children's department, and even further to the tasty delights of the tearoom, meant stepping into the elevator, since George Court's building construction had precluded any installation of escalators.[149] With the clang of all doors securely shut, came the rousing call of 'ground floor — going up?' and the lift was under way. But wait — the lift was stopping already! First Bob had to go 'shopping with mother' through the mysterious domain of the women's frock salon.

CHAPTER TWO

First Floor — Mantle Showroom, Millinery, Manchester and Mercery

'I had bought some of the latest material, *everglaze*, which was all the rage, and a pattern from the D.I.C., and I was sewing by hand a dress to wear some night to the dance', wrote Janet Frame, recalling her efforts to become a follower of fashion in mid-1940s Dunedin.[1] Large department stores like the DIC took pains to offer the 'stuff as dreams are made on' to their principal customers — women. The fabric of department store history is richly patterned with studies of women and their central role in the culture of the stores. Women regarded the stores as the focus of all that was glamorous and fashionable, offering abundant goods and services that would enhance their own lives, and those of their families and friends. There were those who, having seen the children off to school, might leave the sweeping, vacuuming, dusting, and washing, and head to town on tram or bus. They could catch up with the latest exciting arrivals at as many department stores as possible, and still be home by 3 p.m. There were, too, the office and shop workers who used their lunch-hour for a bite to eat, then walked the main street checking out the stores' display windows or dashing in to buy a pair of stockings or gloves. Other women would catch up with friends or fellow club-members at a department-store tearoom and spend some leisure time shopping on the way. Women were the shoppers whose level of consumption was most affected by the

OPPOSITE: A charming model shows a Beath's evening gown in 1923.
PHOTOGRAPH: H. H. CLIFFORD. 1980.175.195, CANTERBURY MUSEUM.

store's efforts to introduce the most up-to-date items available, whether in clothing or in housewares.[2]

Many women also worked in the stores. From the other side of the showroom counter, one Auckland assistant shared her memories:

I began work in the mantle showroom as an eighteen year old in 1934. Feather boas and feather capes were still 'in' then, but I was very glad when they went 'out' a few years later. They were stored in tissue paper and you had to watch very carefully that you didn't break the spines of the feathers as you handled them. The waist-length capes came in different colours, but mainly in white, as debutantes used to wear them.[3]

From their beginnings, successful department stores and their staff needed to be ever alert to what might be 'in' or 'out'. They aimed always to be one step ahead in presenting the latest styles, whether in garments, millinery, fabrics, accessories or cosmetics. In 1910 newspaper journalist 'Tohunga' had enthused, 'in such great department stores as that of Messrs Smith & Caughey, everything that ladies need for their dressings . . . are gathered . . . from the ends of the earth and from every country under the sun'.[4] Ten years later, a copywriter in no doubt about Napier's status à la mode reassured customers that the 'House of Blythes is essentially in a class of its own as the fashion centre of the East Coast. Stocks . . . are imported direct from the world's greatest houses, and bear, in every case the hallmark of fashion and quality.'[5]

Department stores were providers of the materials — silks and cottons, woollens and linens — from which clothing could be made. In early years, fabric bought at the counter was usually transformed into made-to-measure garments in the store's own workrooms. Many still chose dress lengths from the store's mercery department and had their own model garments made up by a dressmaker, but an increasing number created their own individual styles with the aid of paper patterns and sewing machines, also marketed by the stores. Gradually, however, women began to purchase from the ever-multiplying racks and drawers of ready-made clothing offered by department stores.

For the would-be home sewer like Janet Frame, or for the woman who employed someone to create her clothes, there could be 'untold satisfaction and infinite pleasure in buying Evening Frockings at Beath's' for a special occasion. 'The range of choice so wide, the colourings so pretty and varied. Soft draping Silks and Satins, gloriously toned

Tissues, Crystal Crepes, Velvets and Velveteens. Specially selected for their effectiveness in happy surroundings. Choose at Beath's and choose correctly.'[6] Also in 1925 the mercery department of the DIC in Dunedin offered to sweep away the bleakness of winter with their imported materials: 'Colour riots in silk. Just picture Silks in a mass of flaming Marigolds! Larkspurs hobnobbing with Delphiniums! And Eastern design in a hundred schemes of soft and vivid tones.'[7] Such bright, cheerful images could easily catch a woman's imagination when she was shopping for a new spring wardrobe.

Since women are integral to department store history, their story is significant in tracking the somewhat uneven pathway of New Zealand stores from their zenith in the mid-1920s, to the challenges of the 1960s. Yet through these decades of New Zealand's social history, the voices of women customers, though clearly present, were somewhat muted. Their narrative is not one of temptation, seduction and desire, as Gail Reekie

A grand mannequin parade of autumn fashions held in March 1926 in Farmers' showroom, Christchurch. IMG0079, CHRISTCHURCH CITY LIBRARY.

claimed in her study of Australian stores.[8] Women's relationships with the stores speak rather of the great enjoyment and variety that all the stores offered, even through tough times, and of the trust that women placed in the stores, which were perceived as not only arbiters of fashion, but also as reliable and customer-friendly firms, offering many services. The gleaming thread of promise spun by department stores, which wound its confident way through all the years of plenty as well as those of hardship and shortages, was undoubtedly the magic strand of fashion. It featured in their stylish advertisements, in lively and entertaining mannequin parades and in vibrant and ever-changing promotions in the store's display windows; it glowed with light and colour, like the under-counter trays massed with breath-taking silk flowers on a grey afternoon.

Fashion's ever-changing decrees were seen by the stores as a sure foundation on which to build an increasing volume of sales and of rising profits.[9] 'Fashion imparts to merchandise a value over and above its intrinsic worth', stated one writer in 1908, and 'imbues with special desirability goods which would excite only languid interest.'[10] According to Jerome Koerber, decorator and display manager at the store of Strawbridge and Clothier in Philadelphia, 'there is not another word that means so much to the department store as *Fashion*'.[11] New Zealand stores shared some of the vision of providing the latest in styles for women; but there were also significant differences. The local fashion scene had to contend with difficult obstacles, some of which they could occasionally turn to their advantage.

The most obvious difficulty was their geographic distance from major world centres. Sited as they were on the farthest shores of fashion, with the occasional devastating loss of precious cargo through disasters at sea, New Zealand stores nevertheless sought to establish and publicise their clear linkage with the international centres where style trends were launched. As they consolidated and enlarged their businesses, New Zealand department stores prided themselves on their ability to source the latest fashions from overseas, as well as from local suppliers.[12] Whether a knitted 'Garibaldi', a 'Nobby Choker Necklet, specially designed for the wearers of shingled hair', Christian Dior's 'New Look' or Italian post-war chic, local department stores aimed to be among 'the first with the latest, always'.[13]

Appreciative viewers at a fashion parade in James Smith's tearoom in the 1950s.

In-house model Mavis Ross (Lee) photographed in the latest French millinery styles
for Farmers' fashion catalogue, c.1927. MAVIS ROSS COLLECTION, R. LEE.

George Court's implied an authority based on close liaison with international style,
saying 'Paris tells us that Cape Suits and ensembles are the order of the moment . . . and
at George Court's you will find them!'[14] The DIC in Wellington offered exclusive model
hats from Paris at half price in 1920:

> These Paris-created Models are just a few left over from the DIC stock and if you were
> privileged to go direct to Paris to buy your Hat you could not buy prettier styles than those
> we are now offering. What an opportunity to own a smart, exclusive model Hat originated
> by Master Parisian Designers and to buy it for the price of just an ordinary style. There are
> only twelve models for sale so please come early and make your choice; lucky the woman
> who is fortunate in securing one. See them today. 7 guineas to 5 guineas.[15]

A few years later, Kirkcaldie & Stains invited their customers to see 'The "Ensemble"
Suit. The Vogue of the Moment. The latest Parisian Styles are reflected in these
very smart suits which we have just received from our London buyers.'[16] Beath's of

Teams of dressmakers and tailoresses were kept busy in department-store workrooms. A group of staff from Smith & Caughey's alteration room, c.1920. J. DEY.

Christchurch, 'The Home of Lovely Things', had 'frocks for any and every function. Delightful House Frocks . . . Coats and Costumes so very smart. Paris finds expression, London interprets the style, New York contributes much that is unique. You quickly see what you want at Beath's.'[17] Arthur Barnett Ltd in Dunedin advertised 'Fifty Thousand Pounds worth of Model Frocks, Coats, Costumes, Dresses and incidentals . . . the whole magnificent stock was personally selected by our Miss Bunbury when in London, Paris and New York on her recent visit'.[18]

Throughout the 1920s and 1930s, trips abroad were regularly undertaken by department store buyers, who worked in conjunction with those overseas firms engaged to purchase on the stores' behalf. By 1923, John Court in Auckland proudly listed buying offices in London, New York and Yokohama.[19] Smith & Caughey's regularly continued to send buyers to London, New York and European capitals, until import restrictions were imposed in 1938.[20] In 1933 they advertised 'an exceptional exhibition of exclusive Spring frocks, Coats, etc. personally selected by our Miss Paterson in London, Paris, Vienna, and New York. A cordial invitation to all to visit this exclusive Exhibition. Please note: we do not display exclusive models. Ask to see them.'[21] Jean Howe (née Burton) remembered Smith & Caughey's fashion buyer travelling overseas twice a year and bringing a selection of garments back. Some models would be sold directly on the showroom floor, while others were used for copying by the 20 or so women employed in the store's workroom. Debenham and Freebody's and other English catalogues and publications were used to provide ideas for fashion garments. Showroom assistants cut out pictures of garments and pasted them into brown paper books, from which the buyer selected ideas to be made up either by their workroom staff or local manufacturing firms.[22]

Overseas fashion experts were recruited by local firms. After Milne & Choyce embarked upon their 1920s building programme, Mrs Lightband of London was engaged for the showroom at a salary of £8 a week, leaving for New Zealand about the end of June 1922.[23] This important appointment took place over a year ahead of that department's opening on 21 August 1923. Occupying significant space in the first of Milne & Choyce's newly completed floors, the showroom offered 'Springtime Fashions, Millinery and Flowers [which] may be inspected at leisure in harmonious surroundings

Farmers' 1927 parade of imported French fashions in their first tearoom. MAVIS ROSS COLLECTION, R. LEE.

that embody features entirely new to this city'. The showroom was promoted as the store's major attraction.[4]

Despite the glamour attached to overseas styles and personnel, there were difficulties stocking the mantle showroom from overseas. A quantity of frocks and accessories specially imported from France remained unsold after Farmers' 1927 Spring Fashion parade. These exclusive fashions were offered first to shareholders at half price, and then to the general public at the same markdown.[25] Milne & Choyce directors fielded early complaints about the showroom's wares, and suggested, after negotiations with their London office of Bickley and Bell, that the only satisfactory remedy for the problem was to send their own buyers to the United Kingdom.[26] Soon after, the directors confidently stated 'notwithstanding the fact that we are established in London, Paris, New York, and Toronto, the wisdom of sending Heads of Departments possessing intimate knowledge of this business to assist in the purchase of our local requirements, has been more than justified. Without doubt, this co-ordination of effort has kept us thoroughly up-to-date, and is attributable to the increase of business.'[27] For another store, the wisdom of importing outfits such as the latest waterproof 'AMERICAN CHIC' swimsuit in 'Pebble Crepe Rubber' (a possible forerunner of the wet-suit), might well have been questioned. The directive was to 'start the Swimming Season in the right mood with this gay and new little American Swim Suit . . . Very original is the little detachable skirt that fits so neatly to the figure. There is only a limited quantity, so choose yours early! Medium Size only — Price 19/11.'[28] Only a relatively small number of these clammy swimsuits was imported, a wise move for George Court's, until the summer market was tested.

Co-ordinating purchasing efforts with other New Zealand department stores offered economic advantages. These groupings could help to counter the difficulties of distance from world centres of fashion. In 1936, John Court Ltd combined with Invercargill's H. & J. Smith and House and Daking in Hamilton, to form an overseas buying group, later strengthened by linking several more of New Zealand's city and provincial department stores under the banner of United Stores Ltd.[29] Some stores preferred to operate independently; others worked through links with Australian stores. At the end of 1937, Milne & Choyce terminated their longstanding arrangement with Bickley and Bell of London, and entered into a trans-Tasman buying agreement with David Jones Ltd of Sydney. By June 1939, however, 'in view of the constantly changing position, the necessity of sending further buyers to Australia was also discussed'.[30] By the 1940s, buyers' trips even across the Tasman were few and far between, replaced by journeys around New Zealand. 'Several buyers had made a trip south and had been quite successful . . . [but] stocks were steadily going down.'[31]

Even trans-Tasman buying had its difficulties. George Court's reduced the price of their stock of 'Medici style, Wallaby fur collars in Sable or Skunk', from 11s 9d to 8s 11d each, in mid-winter 1935.[32] By the end of July they had hopped down to the 'Bargain Thursday' price of 5s 11d and, nearly a month later, in the last week of the sale, before the new spring fashions were to be presented, the Wallaby fur collars still lurked at rock-bottom prices.[33]

As the difficulty of selling stocks of such eclectic accessories indicated, the local market for women's fashion garments was not large when compared with its overseas counterparts. New Zealand's main urban centres, although steadily growing, were much smaller than neighbouring Sydney and Melbourne. While department stores were able to negotiate lower prices through the bulk ordering of merchandise, as turnover grew larger the potential for losses increased concomitantly. 'The higher the fashion, the greater the risk', ruefully stated one erstwhile department-store managing director.[34]

Since the early days of New Zealand's settlement, several women department store founders, in their small but smart drapery establishments, had taken those risks and had been among the arbiters of fashion for their own sex. Overseas, women were not the prime initiators of department stores, but New Zealand's colonial development provided an environment in which women could play a pioneering role in growing small but successful enterprises. The unique involvement of women in the founding of some of New Zealand's major department stores, including several of the surviving *grandes dames*, was little recognised. As Erik Olssen noted, the societal pressure on women was to conform to the notion of separate spheres — women were to be occupied by home duties and the role of scientific motherhood.[35] Female leaders in commerce did not fit easily into that prescriptive ideology. An 1898 account of 'Smith and Caughey's Establishment: the Largest Soft Goods Emporium in New Zealand' is a paeon of praise to the great and famous partnership of William H. Smith and Andrew C. Caughey, but makes no mention of Marianne Smith (née Caughey) and her significant role in establishing the firm (she also became one of the directors of the store).[36] An *Auckland Star* feature on Milne & Choyce's diamond jubilee in 1926 — at which time it 'gave employment to over 400 people' — noted 'it is sixty years ago since the firm . . . commenced business in an unpretentious manner'. It continued: 'few people in those early days could have visualized the palace that was to arise from so small a beginning. But there were keen, solid men at the head of the firm and their motto "The chain lengthens and strengthens" has indeed proved apt.'[37] Sisters Mary Jane and Charlotte Milne's major contribution in establishing the firm was overlooked, as was the importance of Mary Jane's ongoing involvement with Milne & Choyce Ltd, even after her retirement in her seventieth year in 1909.[38]

The success of other New Zealand's department stores, as they evolved from small millinery and drapery shops, reflected the vision and hard work of their women founders. In the small settlement of Wellington, an enterprising Miss Taylor established Te Aro House in 1845, on-selling it to the Misses Smith, from whom James Smith purchased the small building in 1866. Consolidated and enlarged, the business moved further along Cuba Street to become an important department store. Also virtually unknown was the early involvement of Mrs Bain, a widow, who opened a drapery shop in Dunedin early in 1849. After her marriage to businessman and politician J. Patterson, the business changed hands several times and was bought by John Ross and Robert Glendining in 1862.[39] Before long this firm was to become Brown, Ewing, one of the city's most stylish department stores.

The latest fashions in headgear were important to style setters in far-flung, colonial society. Christchurch was the destination of Esther Clarkson, a milliner, who emigrated from Dunstable in Bedfordshire, a town noted for the manufacture of straw for hats and bonnets. In 1854, with her husband, David, she set up an enterprise that became known as Dunstable House, importing and creating millinery for sale from a cottage at the centre of the present site of Ballantynes store, with business further expanded by William Pratt who bought it in 1864, before later purchase by John Ballantyne.[40] Almost as soon as the Milne family arrived in Auckland from Northern Ireland in 1863, 23-year-old daughter Mary Jane Milne started work as head milliner in a local store. With Charlotte, she bought the stock of Wilson's small millinery and drapery shop on the corner of Wyndham and Albert Streets. They opened their new business M. & C. Milne's on 3 July 1867, supplying stylish, good quality hats and bonnets to the smart set of Auckland.[41]

Early in 1880, Marianne Smith arrived in Auckland from Belfast with her husband William Henry Smith and opened Smith's Cheap Drapery Warehouse, on the corner of Queen and Alexandra (now Airedale) Streets.[42] William joined her in 1881 as the

Queen Street, Auckland, pre-1884, showing John Smith's drapery shop, later bought by Smith & Caughey Ltd in 1891, after they had leased it for some years. There seems no evidence of horse-tram lines up Queen Street and left into Wellesley Street West, thence to the Ponsonby Reservoir. This first section was opened in August 1884. 01179, ALEXANDER TURNBULL LIBRARY, WELLINGTON.

business strengthened. In October 1882, Marianne's brother Andrew Clarke Caughey, a draper, who had arrived in New Zealand a little earlier than the Smiths and who had been a minister in the Wesleyan Church for almost three years, joined them in the business which was then renamed Smith and Caughey. In 1884, having bought the drapery stock of John Smith (who was not a family member), Smith and Caughey leased his premises on part of their present Queen Street site.[43]

The turn of the century saw Helen Hay Smith join with her younger brother John William Smith as founding partners in H. & J. Smith's retail venture in Invercargill.

They opened a small shop named 'A House of Service' in Dee Street in 1900, selling clothing that they manufactured. The shop was soon enlarged and by 1905 a branch had been opened in Gore. In 1910 both the Invercargill store and the Gore branch moved to larger premises. Helen was appointed managing director in 1912, when the business became a private company. Adjacent property was purchased and new premises built in Invercargill by 1917. Sadly, Helen Smith did not live to see further expansion, as she died in the influenza epidemic of 1918, but her skills as an astute businesswoman were honoured and acknowledged throughout the firm's history.[44]

Whether instigated by women or not, building a flourishing business on the shifting sands of fashion was dependent upon New Zealand's fluctuating economic climate. A shortage of cotton, one outcome of the American Civil War, resulted in difficulties for many drapery and department stores worldwide. The sharp depression which New Zealand experienced in the mid-1860s brought tight times for small businesses such as Mary Jane and Charlotte Milne's newly opened Auckland shop, and for William Pratt's Dunstable House in Christchurch.[45] Yet even within New Zealand, these difficulties could vary with local conditions. As Wellington was the site of a newly formed and thriving capital city, business continued unaffected, even buoyant, for Kirkcaldie & Stains' drapery shop.

Another major economic depression followed in the 1880s. Even in such economically straitened years, however, there were some advantages of time and distance. A Smith & Caughey's catalogue, published in 1888–89, drew particular attention to the fact that spring and summer goods in their 'Silk, Dress, Mantle, Millinery, Ribbon, and Fancy Departments . . . contain many lots secured by their buyers at the end of the London season at exceptionally low prices which will be sold by S. & C. much under current rates'. This thrifty and cost-effective policy of buying 'close-outs' cheaply at the end of the Northern Hemisphere season, in order to on-sell in New Zealand as the southern season began six months later, was continued by other firms as well as Smith & Caughey's, who maintained a policy of 'cutting our cloth to fit our means'.[46] New Zealand may have been the first in the world to greet the dawn of each day, but there were distinct economic advantages in being the last link in the global fashion-chain.

Even this was not enough to counter the effects of the Great Depression, though. During the years following the financial crash of 1929, trends in clothing and millinery became 'leaner, economical and conservative', reflecting straitened times.[47] In the

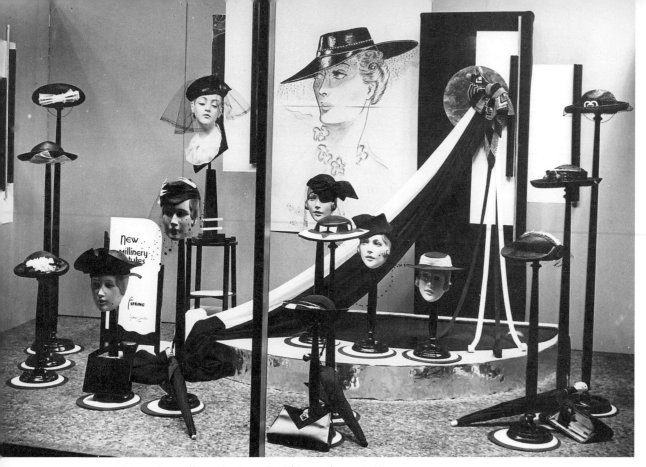

New spring millinery in James Smith's window, c.1930s. PA COLLECTION 3332 – 03 33, ALEXANDER
TURNBULL LIBRARY, WELLINGTON.

gloom of the late winter of 1933, Smith & Caughey's sought to place themselves as 'the
earliest with the newest' in spring millinery. While encouraging customers with the
information that 'prices are extremely low . . . inspection is cordially invited . . . quietly
walk through and view the great exhibition of Spring goods in all departments', the
polite reassurance was given, as always in department stores, that 'no one will be asked
to buy'.[48] A tension is apparent between the implicit urging of customers to buy the
newest in fashion from this department store's variety of merchandise, thus ensuring
its commercial survival, and Smith & Caughey's sensitivity to the financial constraints

faced by many of its patrons when considering the purchase of such an extravagance as a new hat. A year later at their winter 'Fair', Smith & Caughey advertised their finest fur-felt ready-to-wear hats reduced to 9s 11d. At the same time, model hats in fur-felt and velour at George Court's in Karangahape Road were being marked down to 9s 11d, and ready-to-wears to as little as 2s 11d to 4s 11d.[49] Rendell's had '1000 hats to be sacrificed at 3/11 in a one-price clearaway'.[50] If a new hat was an absolute necessity, it paid to shop around.

Hats were *de rigueur* for women in the public domain. Millinery represented consumption at its most conspicuous. Whether frivolous or sophisticated, pretty or tailored, hats were a necessary and important component of women's wardrobes. Some women could afford to be extravagant for, as Queen Elizabeth II's Danish-born milliner Aage Thaarup was later to decree, 'a hat must be "a creation of realities and dreams"'.[51] In spring 1930, with an image of the Eiffel Tower accompanying the advertisement, Rendell's proudly announced that Peggy Vane millinery was being introduced exclusively at their store.[52] Expense notwithstanding, Peggy Vane models were to remain the embodiment of chic for Aucklanders throughout the decades

Aage Thaarup with Auckland model Else Muysenbergh wearing the 'Rangitoto' hat designed in 1952. PHOTOGRAPH: ANGELA LASSIG. *NEW ZEALAND MEMORIES.*

that followed. Aage Thaarup used the city's iconic Rangitoto Island as the inspiration for his first Auckland model hat on a visit in 1954.[53] Between 1953 and 1955 (when he was declared bankrupt), he made five trips to Ballantynes in Christchurch to conduct demonstrations, and to appear at 'Soirées aux Chapeaux'.[54] Smart hats with matching handbags and gloves were a requirement for those who could afford to keep pace with those ever-changing fashion colours and styles.[55] In this, department stores had a distinct advantage over specialty frock shops, for hats and handbags, shoes, hosiery and gloves could all be co-ordinated and selected to match a new outfit without customers having to leave the store.

Gloves, like hats, were an integral component of women's outdoor clothing. 'Gloves are not merely a luxury, they are essential to the well-dressed woman', stated Ballantynes of Christchurch, continuing confidently that 'Ballantynes gloves represent the best output of the leading English and French makers and cannot be excelled for quality and value'.[56] Those who aspired to be properly dressed always appeared in public with hands and heads suitably covered. An old maxim stated that 'a gentlewoman donned her gloves before she opened the door, a lady, before she opened the gate, but a woman put on her gloves while walking up the street'. The ritual of glove-fitting followed a time-honoured procedure. Women customers ceremonially took their places at the counter on high bentwood chairs to be fitted with fine leather gloves in an elaborate procedure involving velvet cushions on which to rest their elbows, as each glove was stretched, dusted inside with talcum powder, and gently and expertly eased on to the hand. Gloves were offered in all colours and forms of leather such as kid, nappa, suede and doeskin. So sought after and scarce were imported leather gloves during the latter years of World War II, that George Court's cheerfully offered women the opportunity to laboriously create their own: 'It's easy to make your own gloves with the aid of a reliable pattern, and these lovely skins that are so wonderfully soft and pliable. Skins vary in price according to size.'[57] Knitted gloves in winter, and fabric or silk gloves in all seasons were an option, but matching leather gloves, handbag and shoes were the epitome of fashion. Their disappearance signalled the passing of a customary rite of service and luxury.

A customer is fitted with new gloves in a department store at the time of the 1953–54 Royal Tour. The lion and the kiwi symbols are both incorporated into the Christmas decorations. IMG 00099, AUCKLAND WAR MEMORIAL MUSEUM LIBRARY.

The smartly dressed woman not only completed her outfit with hat and gloves, but increasingly wore discreet make-up. By the 1920s, the use of cosmetics, formerly considered 'fast' and unladylike, was being accepted and publicly promoted. In 1926, '"Phyllis Earle" beauty preparations from Europe' were advertised at Milne & Choyce. The requisite overseas experts were there to advise: 'In attendance will be two experienced Beauty Culturalists, direct from "Mayfair" Salons, London.'[58] Women were being encouraged to adopt this modern practice and to purchase cosmetics. 'Do you use "make-up"?' inquired an article in the January 1927 issue of the New Zealand women's magazine, the *Mirror*. The writer continued 'the woman who is "above" a judicious use of cosmetics might with value reflect that she is in consequence below the standard of beauty and charm she might easily achieve were her ideas of life a little less narrow'. Part of that charm involved 'not forgetting to apply just a suspicion of colour [rouge] to your chin and the tips of your ears (if you have an Eton crop)'.[59] By 1930, Phyllis Earle Beauty Aids were available at Beath's in Christchurch, the DSA, Dunedin, and James Smith's, Wellington, as well as Milne & Choyce in Auckland.[60]

In the 1930s, cosmetic departments in the stores reflected the tremendous growth of the industry in the United States.[61] Perfume and toiletry counters were being relocated adjacent to the main doors, to attract women customers as they entered. A January 1930 *Evening Post* advertisement for Kirkcaldie & Stains' 'Accessories for the Race Ensemble' included beauty products and firmly stated 'If they come from Kirkcaldie's they are correct'. Toiletries listed included not only complexion soap, 'solidified' lavender water, perfume, and eau de Cologne, but also face powder and creams, all well-known lines imported from Europe and England — Dubarry, Houbigant, Morny and Yardley.[62] In 1932 George Court's announced a special purchase of world-famous toiletries — imported perfumes, powders and fragrant soaps, also from famous European and English manufacturers, Yardley, Roger & Gallet, Piver, and Grossmith.[63] J. Grossmith & Sons set out to capture 'All the allure of the Magic East' in perfumes with exotic names such as 'Phūl-Nānā' and 'Shem-el-Nessim' for a generation that had thrilled to the shocking delights of E. M. Hull's novel *The Sheik*, and continued to be fascinated by the romantic and exotic east.[64] Some American cosmetic brand names were also being

An early window display of Paul Duval cosmetics in the DIC, Christchurch.
PHOTOGRAPH: F. E. MCGREGOR. 1982.122.5, CANTERBURY MUSEUM.

advertised. Pompeian Beauty products, from Cleveland, Ohio, including lipstick and rouge, had already featured in 1920s advertisements.[65] The continuing search for a long-lasting lipstick saw Milne & Choyce present a 1935 advertisement for 'Tattoo — the new indelible lipstick. Smartness demands that lips be tattoed instead of coated with paste.'[66] George Court's also promoted the new lip colour: 'TATTOO your lips — four shades like lipstick — let it set, then wipe it off'.[67] Lipstick was here to stay.

Already, world-famous cosmetic brands were becoming familiar to New Zealand women. Stores confidently advertised their links with selected purveyors of beauty, sometimes jostling for their positions as suppliers of a particular line; Ballantynes offered Cyclax products in 1933.[68] In that same year, Milne & Choyce claimed that since 1920 they had been the sole distributors of Elizabeth Arden toiletries in Auckland. In 1927, however, Elizabeth Arden's Venetian toilet preparations were advertised as available from Smith & Caughey's in Auckland, Kirkcaldie & Stains in Wellington

Demonstration for Max Factor cosmetics on the ground floor of Milne & Choyce c.1950.
PHOTOGRAPH: WALTER J. THOMPSON. REAY CLARKE COLLECTION, J. GRANT.

and Beath & Co. Ltd, Christchurch.[69] In 1935, one advertisement stated that Helena Rubinstein beauty preparations were obtainable from Smith & Caughey's; another announced that John Court Ltd held stocks of those 'exceptionally low priced Pompeian toiletries'.[70] Demonstrations of Harriet Hubbard Ayer products were given in Milne & Choyce's 'Toilet Section' by Audrey Macfarlane, 'Beauty Counselor for the famous toilet preparations'. Max Factor make-up was stocked by department stores McGruers Ltd in Wanganui, the DIC in Wellington, and John Court in Auckland.[71] The latter firm also offered free make-up demonstrations 'by Miss Lynette Stewart — coming directly from Hollywood after 6 months personal tuition from Max Factor [she] will reveal to you all the beauty secrets of Hollywood's lovely screen stars'.[72] Many women took the opportunity to attend in-store instruction sessions, for they enjoyed using make-up and considered it enhanced their personal charm.

New Zealand department stores occasionally promoted local beauty products without internationally known names. Local glamour was glamour nonetheless. Under a photograph of the couple's wedding, *Herald* readers in 1935 were informed that 'Mr Cyril Ritchard and his bride, Miss Madge Elliott, have just returned to Auckland from their honeymoon to commence their season at His Majesty's':

> Miss Madge Elliott, the famous Musical Comedy Actress co-starring with Mr Cyril Ritchard in 'Roberta' which commences at His Majesty's this evening, HAS KINDLY CONSENTED TO OPEN A DEMONSTRATION of New Zealand's World Famed Beauty Treatments — The 'Hinemoa' Facial Pack and 'Zo-Glo' face powder at George Court's at 3 pm to-morrow Thursday. Miss Elliot will open the Demonstration (which is being held in the new Toilet Section, just inside the main doors) . . . and will then accept a casket of 'Zo-Glo' products. Writing of the amazing properties of these unique products Miss Elliott says 'I find your "Zo-Glo" Beauty Powder and "Hinemoa Mud Pack" exceedingly good . . . "Zo-Glo" Preparations are delightful to use'. Yours sincerely, Madge Elliott (Signed).[73]

The bright lights of show business did not meet with approval from everyone. Delighted crowds flocked to see Thelma McMillan, a mantle showroom assistant from Arthur Barnett's department store in Dunedin, and the winner of the first Miss New Zealand contest in November 1926.[74] Among the prizes won by attractive Thelma was the offer of a Hollywood film test, which her mother insisted she turn down.[75]

A John Court window display of 'Classic' winter fashion of the 1940s with handbags, hats and gloves 'at the ready'. Classic garments were manufactured in New Zealand. PHOTOGRAPH: WALTER J. THOMPSON. REAY CLARKE COLLECTION, J. GRANT.

By the 1940s luxury items such as cosmetics and perfumes had a lower profile in department-store advertising, with some imported lines of toilet items, such as talcum powder, virtually unobtainable. Although department stores world-wide shared the problems of how to display and promote the latest in fashion through difficult economic times, in New Zealand government efforts to control imports and encourage local secondary industry brought particular difficulties to department-store managers, buyers and staff — as well as to their women customers.

At the beginning of 1939 Milne & Choyce's Board of Directors reported that 'Import Controls granted licences for the six months ending 30 June equivalent to 39% of the amount of our application'.[76] In 1940 the men on Farmers' Board of Directors regarded with alarm the effect the 'continued import restrictions and new financial regulations will have on the company's operations during the coming year'.[77] New Zealand department-store stores had entered upon an era of austerity. For women customers seeking the latest in fashion or new linen for the home, the challenge of shopping within an increas-

Wartime fashions for women at the DIC, Wellington. 15034, ALEXANDER TURNBULL LIBRARY, WELLINGTON.

ingly narrowing range of merchandise had begun. Not only were severe import restrictions imposed, but as soon as New Zealand entered World War II, price stabilisation was established, and regulations set in place to enforce its measures.[78] Gordon Parry noted that for the DIC 'import restrictions . . . meant a decline in the volume of business . . . The era of intervention politics had begun.'[79]

In the mid-1930s, department stores had confidently pronounced on the latest fashion requirements, reinforcing their status as arbiters by their instructions about what was appropriate: 'What you'll wear this Spring can be seen at Farmers'.[80] As stocks dwindled, the very size and scope of department-store showrooms, with their numerous racks, trays and drawers full of clothing, their displays on mannequins and behind glass doors, all of which had previously ensured their dominance in the fashion scene, served to emphasise the noticeably reduced stock.[81]

In 1944 one mantle showroom attendant reported that, whereas formerly customers could ask for several frocks to be sent to them on approval, women now had to come in and try them on in the store.[82] As well as there being fewer garments from which to make a selection, from May 1942 coupons were needed to complete the transaction, and clothing vied with household linen for those precious allocations. Each person's allowance had to cover not only clothing and shoe requirements, but also cotton or linen goods for home use. According to Mr A. D. Bell, Chairman of Farmers' Board of Directors, 'the government's action in making customers use clothing coupons to purchase Manchester and household linen goods would prove a great hardship'.[83]

The stores' manchester departments took their name from the Lancashire city that had been the chief centre of nineteenth-century British cotton manufacturing. Department stores had always prided themselves on being the main providers of the bed and table linen that helped to make homes attractive and comfortable. Those important ranges, generally sourced from manufacturing centres in Great Britain, Europe and the United States, were piled on shelves in crisply folded and packaged stacks, or draped on display stands, so that prospective buyers could readily feel their quality and note their size. They included white cotton or linen sheets and pillowcases, towels of all descriptions, damask, linen and cotton tablecloths and napkins, tea-towels and tray-cloths. For Christmas 1929 James Smith's — 'The House of the Present' — suggested linen as a gift for women: '5,000 pieces of Beautiful Christmas napery displayed for your O.K. We have opened a new and larger Fancy Linen Section on the ground floor. Here all the novel Household Linens you could imagine are displayed for your approval, and with us too you will find a friendly Christmas spirit of courtesy and help even to your smallest wants.'[84] As early as 1929 Kirkcaldie & Stains were advertising that 'Colour has been introduced into Sheetings and Kirkcaldies offer their "Kayaness" Sheets in these soft shades — Pink, Blue, Mauve and Daffodil'.[85] This was more than a 'brief encounter' with coloured bed-linen; in 1938 Smith & Caughey were still advertising pink, green, blue or primrose sheets and pillowcases at sale price.[86] Wartime put an end to these colourful deviations.

At marriage, women assumed responsibility for providing an ample supply of linen including sheets and towels and, from that time onward, the ongoing selection and replacement of such household goods were among the duties of a housewife. A 'Simple Trousseau for a Present-Day Bride' from the Girls' Own Annual published at the end of 1918 added an astonishing assemblage of linen to a long list of clothing requirements. A prospective English bride needed: 'Six pairs of cotton double sheets, 2 pairs of linen double sheets, 6 pairs of single sheets, 1 dozen linen pillow slips, 2 dozen bath towels, 1 dozen face towels, 4 large dinner cloths, 2 dozen dinner napkins, 6 or 8 tea cloths, 2 dozen tea serviettes . . . 1 dozen floor cloths . . . 2 or 3 dozen dusters'. The inventory continued, with many more items of all sorts listed by the dozens. [87]

While such a list might exceed the requirements of most New Zealand brides, nevertheless trousseau linen, stored traditionally in a 'glory box' or 'bottom drawer', needed to be collected before marriage. Women trusted department stores to provide them with the necessary selection of attractive and hard-wearing goods at the best possible prices. Farmers' also offered wooden or fabric-covered 'Glory Boxes — Happy choice for any girl'.[88] Ballantynes advertised sets of bridal linen which included the obligatory 'Sheets, Pillowcases, Towels, Dining Cloths with Napkins to match, Quilts, Tea Cloths, Glass Cloths, Bath Mats etc.' Prices ranged from Set No. 1 at £15, to Set No. 6 at £31 10s.[89] Neighbouring Beath's confidently stated that 'Brides come to Beath's — naturally. The Linen Section at Beath's is a source of infinite pleasure to lovers of pure linens and of lasting satisfaction to buyers because of their exceptional quality. Good linens are the pride of the housewife, and it is Beath's pleasure to provide the very finest linens that the world produces.'[90] American embroidered pillowcases, Venetian lace pillow shams, and fine embroidered Madeira linen goods were among the items available. In 1938, Milne & Choyce were advertising their 'famous £15 trousseau' but by 1940, with import restrictions already beginning to affect supplies, George Court was offering to provide brides with a set of trousseau linen 'from 9 guineas'.[91]

As well as the inevitable task of laundering and starching the linen and cotton goods, some of the items in these collections for new brides, including dusters, dish and floor cloths, reflected the hard domestic work expected of most women. 'Good housewifery demands a linen cupboard replete with plenteous supplies of all that is necessary in household linen.'[92] Well might department stores introduce housewives to the 'Chelsea Smock — even into those hours devoted daily to household tasks comes a new smartness . . . [for] the protection of your new Spring Frocks. Made from splendid wearing, fast colour check gingham — collar, cuffs and pockets finished with white and a large bow of black silk at the throat.'[93] Others offered 'smart smocks that give you purposeful poise. Designed to take the irk out of housework . . . printed to give you colour charm'![94] Farmers' presented 'Beautiful, dutiful cottons [smocks] keep you pretty while you work', and Smith & Caughey's 'Novelty waist aprons in floral washing prints 4/6 — 1 coupon'.[95]

An amazing early-morning crowd queueing to buy towels outside Miller's department store in 1944 at a time when towels were virtually unprocurable. MILLER COLLECTION. 1997.321.1, CANTERBURY MUSEUM.

After years of hard wear, and regular boiling in the copper, squeezing through the wringer, visits to the bag-wash, linen inevitably wore out. 'Re-stock your linen cupboard during House Linen Week', instructed John Court Ltd. 'Prices are so low on many needed items that every economic woman will appreciate the advisability of laying in a full supply.'[96] Depression years brought the 'turning' of sheets, and the creation of household linen from recycled sugar and flour bags.[97] There were, however, relatively cheap replacements offered for those who could afford them. In 1935, for the same price as a special mixed grill — 1s 6d — George Court's advertised a special one-price grouping of 'Reliable British Towels': 'dark towels, so serviceable in the hands of

76

naughty little boys who wash their faces on their towels. Hard spun gripping towels, for a good rub down, such as Father revels in. Towels of soft comfy finish, much preferred by Mother and the girls.'[98]

By 1944, with import restrictions and war shortages reducing supplies to a minimum, new towels of any description were eagerly sought after. Queues formed at the news that cotton or linen goods were available in a particular department store. 'There's a queue at John Court's, extending out the door, chattering women gripping dog-eared ration books. The words "bed linen" are afloat. Your glory box needs more sheets, but there is no time to join the ranks today, and anyway, when you eventually reach the counter the meagre wartime stocks will have been exhausted.'[99] New Zealand farmers were growing linen-flax to help Britain's war effort, but it was not destined to produce fine linen sheets or tablecloths for local households.[100] If they could be bought, a pair of double sheets took ten precious coupons at George Court's, and a pair of single sheets, seven coupons.[101] To stock the increasingly bare home linen cupboards, unbleached cotton sheeting could sometimes be bought as an alternative to pure white. Hardwearing and cheaper though they might be, such sheets never attained the snowy whiteness promised by Rinso, Taniwha or Persil soap powder advertisements. In mid-1945, with the end of hostilities almost in view, Ballantynes proudly took a full page advertisement for a large stock of English-made Horrockses sheets and pillowcases offered for sale '"in spite of the war". Large double bed sheets were three guineas a pair (11 coupons) and envelope-style pillowcases 4/9 (one coupon each).'[102]

Shortages, whether of linen, clothes or cosmetics, were something that New Zealand women made the best of, and accepted pragmatically as part of the general war effort. The war, not government policy, was responsible for some difficulties, for it was helpfully explained by the stores that 'even without import restrictions, stocks of that eau-de-Cologne would not be available because the company factory that produced it has been bombed out of existence by the Allied Air Forces'.[103]

Department stores, like other advertisers, linked the promise of peace with the re-establishment of those lines of consumer goods formerly available: 'When Victory Comes . . . you'll want to do a lot of things . . . to fill your car with petrol and gad about . . . to buy unreservedly the things you like. But when you tire of too much celebrating you'll welcome the homely things that have remained unchanged in a changing world.'[104] There was hope and expectation that things would be different, despite all the difficulties that the stores and their customers alike had experienced.

A Milne & Choyce advertisement, published just two days before the first atomic bomb was dropped on Hiroshima, trod a careful line between supporting austerity in the name of the war effort and encouraging its clientele to come into the store and spend on their spring wardrobes:

What are they wearing in the three fashion centers? . . . In Paris, clothes are soberer than under the occupation, when fashion went frilly to taunt the Huns. Apparel is unrationed, steeply priced, and still has bulky lines — perhaps for warmth. In London, wardrobes are crippled by privation. Designers' hands are tied. Yet in spite of rationing and 'austerity' styles British women have proved how well they can 'make-do'. In New York, order L-85 limits the length of jacket and sweep of skirt. It is no serious problem; women love the narrow silhouette. Shoes alone are rationed. As in other great cities, American fashion reflects a mood impatient with fuss. This Spring, new Milne & Choyce fashions are also far from frivolous. Our buyers have traveled the Dominion. Imports are at the limit of our licences. Merchandise assembled is up to the minute; but as always . . . quality is the keynote.[105]

In the months after the war ended, department stores again assumed the role of advising the latest in fashion for women. Since supplies of some of those long-remembered items like silk scarves might remain elusive for some time, one firm attempted to 'make history by introducing to New Zealand Plastic Scarves. What further proof that George Court's are alive to the present fashion trend in London . . . New York . . . Paris! This very instant plastic fabrics are receiving the acclamation of "Vogue," "Harpers Bazaar" and "Mademoiselle". These triangular headwear scarves in gay florals and discreet self-colours are soft, warm, windproof, waterproof and crease resisting. Really a miracle fabric. See them in our windows and at the neckwear department, 5/11.'[106] To further express the theme of modern scientific progress, the advertisement was accompanied by an illustration of a Bunsen burner, flask and clamp.

As well as plastic, other new fabrics, such as nylon in its many forms, developed during the 1930s, were increasingly available on the world market. New Zealand's import restrictions continued to be imposed with varying degrees of stringency, with wartime pricing regulations replaced by legislation in 1947.[107] Licences were needed for the new, easy-care garment options but also for supplies of classic garments such as Pringle knitwear, with 'limited quantities of Britain's finest woollens just arrived from

A display of Erinore single and double cotton sheets from Northern Ireland in James Smith's window in the 1940s. Coupon requirements are indicated, together with the price, the number of threads per square inch, and the breaking strength of warp and weft. PA COLLECTION 3332, ALEXANDER TURNBULL LIBRARY, WELLINGTON.

Scotland' and Smith & Caughey's exclusive stocks of the '"Pytchley" Famous English Tailored Jodhpurs and Breeches for Ladies and Gentlemen'.[108] A great deal of other merchandise dear to the hearts of women, including fine china, crystal, silverware and household linen as well as shoes, fashion garments and cosmetics, competed for those precious licences. It presented a huge challenge to department store buyers to use their allocations to good effect, balancing innovation and tradition, householders' need to restock basic items, and the desire for luxury goods.

In the post-war years, spirits began to lift in spite of the continuing restrictions. In June 1947 Milne & Choyce brought two guest mannequins by air to Auckland from

Sydney for a Paris fashion parade that raised £1000 for the 'Food for Britain' campaign. In February 1948, despite the fact that New Zealand was heading into autumn, Christian Dior's revolutionary and exciting 'New Look' Spring Collection was flown to New Zealand with guest mannequin Miss New Zealand, Mary Woodward. Farmers' reported in 1950 that its 'first Fashion Parade since the war created tremendous excitement among the feminine population of Auckland'.[109] Ballantynes supplied the selection of 1950 gowns at the presentation of 'Canterbury Centennial Cavalcade of Fashion 1859–1950'. Following their previous year's 'Easter Parade of Practical Fashions', George Court's endeavoured to stimulate interest in their 1952 women's clothing range with 'Five Star Easter Parades' in their tearoom featuring 'MANNEQUIN PARADES OF FASHIONS YOU CAN WEAR. Budget planned creations with an air of dignity and charm inspired by the world's greatest fashion designers in London, Paris and New York.'[110] The following year, George Court's fashion department reported 'a quickening of business which we hope will be maintained' as selling for the Royal Tour functions took priority.[111]

The coronation of Queen Elizabeth in 1953, and her subsequent tour of New Zealand, provided department stores with an opportunity for the display and sales of fashion goods and souvenirs on a grand scale. In Auckland a 'Coronation Collection' of 16 garments from a first showing before the Queen in the Royal Festival Hall, London, together with genuine peers' and peeresses' robes, and one of six models of the coronation coach made for world distribution, were displayed in Milne & Choyce. In Christchurch, special advertising by local department stores reflected the amazing excitement of the occasion, and the great deference due to royalty. Farmers' offered a free flag to all children who came to their store accompanied by an adult, while Ballantynes and Beath's each had their own exclusive Royal Tour silk scarves for sale, together with other Royal Tour mementoes. Hay's was certain that 'Everyone will want a souvenir from Hay's to commemorate the Royal Visit'.[112] Advertisements by Dunedin department stores, however, were more restrained with generally no reference at all to the events gripping the city's attention except for entrepreneurial Arthur Barnett, who had 'your seat for the Royal Visit: Light-weight yet great in strength, folds up neatly to fit

In January 1954, Queen Elizabeth II's motorcade passes James Smith's corner, specially decorated for the Royal Tour. PHOTOGRAPH: DENNIS HODGSON. PA COLLECTION 3332, ALEXANDER TURNBULL LIBRARY, WELLINGTON.

in a coat pocket'. This handy device for those who intended to await the Queen, together with an offer of red, white and blue bunting and a souvenir brooch, featured in the only department store's advertisement in the *Otago Daily Times* which referred to the tour.[113]

For many, the most memorable of the post-war fashion shows was the 1955 visit of four glamorous Italian models, together with the Italian fashion collection of garments reportedly worth £25,000. Following a most successful appearance in Sydney, the entourage travelled first to Auckland, where a late August presentation, 'Italy at Milne & Choyce: Viva Italia', was staged, with a genuine Venetian gondola displayed on the store's first floor, and later to Kirkcaldie & Stains, where the same gondola held pride of place on the ground floor.[114] A lavish gala dinner in the Wellington store's tearoom opened the 'Italy at Kirkcaldie's' season in September, where guests included the Prime Minister's wife, Mrs S. G. Holland, the Deputy Prime Minister K. J. Holyoake with Mrs Holyoake, and members of the diplomatic corps. Italian dishes featured prominently on the menu and the caterer David Thwaites and his staff of 32 needed three weeks to prepare for this spectacular event.[115] The excitement brought by this display of Italian style boosted New Zealand's fashion industry. Although the haute-couture garments modelled in such collections were not for sale in this country, they could be copied locally. Mary Pilkington, an elegant advertising copywriter at Milne & Choyce, who often scripted and compèred that firm's fashion shows, firmly stated her opinion: 'If it weren't good enough for me to buy all my clothes from where I was working in advertising, it wasn't good enough for everybody else'.[116]

Department stores were again selling an exotic range of cosmetics, clothing and accessories. The Paul Duval cosmetic counter in Milne & Choyce was strategically placed facing one of the two main entrances to the store. Here at the 'Powder Bar' among the range of other 'personalised cosmetics', separate glass partitions displayed the many subtle colours of loose powder from which a selection could be made by the consultant in charge. Featuring among the cream, beige, and pink powders were the somewhat alarming sections allocated to mauve and green. In theory, after thorough mixing together in a large and impressive whirring blender, the result was an exclusive shade of face-powder, tailor-made for each woman customer's skin tones.[117] What more personalised beauty aid could anyone want?

By the early 1950s, Farmers' was addressing the needs of its female customers with a campaign entitled: 'Give the Lady what She Wants'. This drive for service and courtesy on the part of the staff was outlined to the Board of Directors in 1953.[118] The

firm's continuing emulation of department stores in the United States, formative in
Robert Laidlaw's early vision for the store, was still being reflected in their patterns of
merchandising, for *Give the Lady What She Wants* was the title of a popular history of
Marshall Field's, first published in 1952.[119] Department stores worldwide had prided
themselves on giving women what they wanted. 'The building is a town in itself',
reported the *Auckland Star* at the time of Milne & Choyce's diamond jubilee in 1926,
'with hundreds of smart assistants in constant attendance on customers.'[120] One
woman, buying a smart suit and hat at Smith & Caughey's for her daughter's wedding
in 1954, found to her dismay after she had left the store that one of the diamonds in her

The ground floor, Milne & Choyce, decorated for a post-war Christmas. The Paul Duval cosmetic
counter (right) has its selection of face-powder tones on view in their glass compartments, while the
streamlined blender sits on top of the counter. The days of paper parcels tied up with string have
long gone, for a sticky-tape dispenser can be seen alongside the cash register (centre).
90.1.37, AUCKLAND WAR MEMORIAL MUSEUM LIBRARY.

engagement ring was missing. Back she went, and together, on their knees, she and an attentive senior staff member from the mantle showroom searched the fitting-room carpet, until the precious tiny stone was found. On such attitudes of courtesy and customer care were the bonds between women and department stores founded.

Women's affectionate and appreciative relationship with their department stores had been tested through hard times. The stores relied on being able to source exciting merchandise from the far corners of the world in their mission to bring New Zealand women their fashion requirements. The ever-present difficulty of being a small and distant 'outpost' of fashion had been constantly addressed, not always with absolute success. Mavis Jaggar-Smith recalled

> I was standing in front of Smith & Caughey's glove counter . . . wearing a pale grey Emma Knuckey suit and a fairly large off-the-face hat. Emma's suits were often a limited edition, and someone else could be wearing a suit like mine. Suddenly a man's arm went around my waist and when I looked up in wonderment, I saw an equally amazed expression on Sir Harcourt Caughey's face. He dropped me like a hot cake and apologized that he had thought I was his wife. I just laughed to myself and was secretly flattered that I looked like Lady Caughey (even from the back). She is such a beautiful lady.[121]

Even through the hard years of the 1930s, the stores had managed to provide varied ranges of imported clothing and linen. The restrictions and shortages of the 1940s and 1950s, and the necessity for local clothing manufacturers to supply a relatively limited market had imposed some limits over the choice of attire and of household linen for women. The stores rallied gallantly, but these problems were to have a long-term effect upon their viability as purveyors of fashion and their efforts to be 'the first with the latest, always'.[122]

After time well spent among the racks of clothing, in front of the changing room mirror, with the help of an experienced and politely helpful showroom assistant, important decisions have been made. It has already been arranged that the store will deliver those larger and bulkier parcels of linen, the box containing that beautiful fashion garment carefully folded in tissue paper, the matching hat, gloves and handbag. It is time to take those patient, but rather bored children up in the lift to their own space on the next floor up: 'Second floor — children's department!'

·

CHAPTER THREE

Second Floor — Children's Department: 'A Million Choices'

When my brother and I were children living in Devonport, in 1927, we loved coming over to town on the Ferry. Then our Mother would take us to the Farmers' shop to play in the children's playground on the top floor. We thought it was Heaven. When Mother was exhausted with watching us, we would all repair to the tearoom on the same floor. We loved seeing Hector the Parrot.[1]

These happy memories of an inveterate department store shopper, now in her eighties, are typical of those cherished by many people throughout New Zealand. Another woman, remembering the joys of December at Kirkcaldie & Stains said: 'In my mind's eye I go back for a brief second every Christmas and it is all magic'.[2] By the 1920s department stores were offering specialised and enchanting new experiences for children.

Farmers' Trading Company was the first department store in New Zealand to provide an all-year-round attraction, deliberately aimed at bringing children and their parents into the store. Advertising promoted Farmers' playground as a veritable children's paradise, which included pedal cars, tricycles, a seesaw, and a high viewing tower complete with telescopes, for the most adventurous.[3] If Santa Claus did not bring the desperately desired pedal car on Christmas Eve, Farmers' provided a sturdy, if somewhat battered, substitute. Heavily used, and patiently waited for while others had their turn, those cars offered for many children a feeling (albeit fleeting) of proud

A purposeful driver at Farmers' roof-top playground c.1940. E. LAURENSON.

automotive ownership, complete with the serious responsibility of filling the vehicle with imaginary fuel from miniature petrol pumps or 'bowsers'. It was an experience that was seldom if ever to be forgotten.

From its opening in 1922, children looked forward to being taken to the 'safe and pleasant surroundings' provided by Farmers' roof-top area, while their parents shopped in comfort, or watched them play.[4] So successful was this open-air, recreational space, that a statement issued in 1927 decreed that only those children accompanied by a parent would be admitted to the playground during the Christmas holidays.[5] An attempt to limit numbers, rather than a safety precaution, it nevertheless strengthened the perception that young children were not independent consumers of goods in their own right: they would always need to be accompanied by someone who could purchase on their behalf.[6]

Farmers' roof-top playground in 1929, with a model railway skirting the edge of the space.
2767, AUCKLAND WAR MEMORIAL MUSEUM LIBRARY.

Indeed for a period of time following World War II, children were not encouraged to enter Kirkcaldie & Stains' Wellington store unless in the company of an adult.[7]

Historians have paid little attention to the role of children as consumers. In general, before 1890, children 'wore, ate, and played with what their parents made or prepared for them', but in the next two decades there was a phenomenal growth in the manufacture and sale of toys, together with clothing for children and babies.[8] This production of an enormous variety of children's goods was linked not only with industrial growth, but also with a much broader change in attitudes to children. For most of the nineteenth century, children were nurtured within an adult society and economy. They worked alongside their parents, or with other adults if apprenticed at an early age, and were part of that adult world. The requirements of a new type of professional, technical and corporate work force, however, required greater levels of education; compulsory schooling legislation removed younger children from the labour force. William Leach argues that by the end of the nineteenth century, psychologists, educators and philosophers began to perceive children as a distinct group within society, with their own defined needs, whereupon academics and researchers instituted the professional study of childhood as a subject in its own right.[9]

While primarily targeting adults, some large overseas department stores, aware of childhood as a 'growth area', seized the opportunity to nurture children's loyalty. In 1902 Marshall Field's Chicago department store inaugurated a 'Children's Day', with its then current manager, Harry Selfridge, telling the staff, 'children are the future customers of this store, and impressions made now will be lasting'.[10] By 1905 children were recognised as important for retailing strategy, whether directly or indirectly.[11] The *Dry Goods Reporter* offered the proposition that 'the children will not spend much money, but they'll spend some. The idea though is not to get them to buy things, but to allow them to see what they want. Then they'll go home and torment their parents to the limit until the thing is purchased.'[12] By 1911, Marshall Field's had adopted Selfridges' policy of encouraging children as future customers. In 1912, they advertised that 'the vast unfolding of the modern child-world is important to this mercantile institution. Not every person realizes that there is a children's demand for merchandise and service. Yet there is naturally. Little people's interests, their desires, their preferences, and rights to merchandise are as strong and as definite as those of any adult portion of the community. An ever-growing attention is being given children and their requirements at Marshall Field and Co.'[13]

Robert Laidlaw of Farmers' Trading Company first travelled to Chicago in 1915 as a young man, calling on the offices of Sears, Roebuck and Montgomery Ward, which were prototypes of the mail-order business he was then operating in New Zealand. Laidlaw would have observed the operations of Marshall Field's while he was in that same city. In 1907, the giant department store had converted its whole fourth level into 'The Children's Floor'. As Farmers' subsequent energetic and innovative efforts to provide special entertainment for the children of Auckland indicate, he too thought it was important to create a space where parents could be active participants in that 'modern child world' of consumption.[14] No doubt James Hay, in turn, was aware of the

A model train with Santa Claus in attendance on the roof-top playground of Hay's department store, Christchurch, in the 1930s. PHOTOGRAPH: F. E. MCGREGOR. 1982.122.6, CANTERBURY MUSEUM.

early success of Farmers' open-air playground in Auckland. At Christmas 1929, only a few weeks after opening, Hay's, 'The Friendly Store' of Christchurch, made a point of welcoming children onto the roof-top playground of its new premises.[15]

Energetic play, as well as shopping with mother, inevitably made children hungry. Whether dining at the Farmers' tearoom, which opened on to the roof-top playground, or further afield in one of the other department store tearooms, eating out was an important part of the ritual of 'going to town'. John Court's daily tearoom lunch menu through the 1930s and 1940s deliberately catered for all family members, offering a 'children's special' meal for four pence. This healthy fare, consisting of a plate of three vegetables, including a scoop of mashed potato with gravy, was served at the table for the same price as a two-stage child's return tram fare from suburban Mt Eden. The novelty of eating out in smart surroundings had its own appeal to children, for whom the trip to town was a special treat.

Department stores also provided rooms where mothers could feed their babies during shopping visits.[16] There were close links with the work of the Royal New Zealand Society for the Health of Women and Children — the Plunket Society — with many of the stores making regular donations to its work. A. C. Caughey's 1923 gift of his family home to the Auckland Branch of the Society for their Karitane Hospital was widely publicised and well documented.[17] Ballantynes advertised its mail-order service in a widely distributed 'Help the Babies' Cookery Book* published in 1924 by the Picton Branch of the Royal New Zealand Society for the Health of Women and Children, with recipes contributed by Lady Jellicoe, the wife of the governor general, and Christina Massey, the prime minister's wife.[18] A 1932 'Bonny Babies' promotion by Arthur Barnett's store in Dunedin went as far as having the matron and sisters from the Redroofs maternity home on display: 'Happy little tots and the baby sisters hold court. One peep into the window and the feeling of depression leaves.'[19] In that same year, Armstrong's of Christchurch offered baby clothes at reduced prices the day before the annual Plunket Day appeal.[20] This reinforcement and extension of consumerism to include altruism and care for others, particularly young family members and babies, deliberately linked department stores with the model of the care-giver, mother as consumer.[21]

One Auckland department store clearly stated its interest in child health. Draper John Rendell and his wife Emily emigrated to New Zealand in 1880 and, after an unsuccessful attempt at farming in the Waikato, John returned to the drapery trade. In 1882 he opened what has been described as 'probably the first baby-wear shop in

Rendell's and George Court's (second building from right) in Karangahape Road, from Pitt Street corner, 1919. PHOTOGRAPH: WINKELMANN, CIO174, AUCKLAND WAR MEMORIAL MUSEUM LIBRARY.

Auckland' on the corner of Pitt Street and Greys Avenue, before a move to the corner of Karangahape Road, near the Prince Edward Theatre.[22] It carried modest stocks of baby and children's wear, much of which was made by Rendell family members.[23] By the early years of the twentieth century, the services that Rendell's offered to mothers who shopped at the firm's later and much larger building in Karangahape Road included monitoring and recording the weight of each child at every visit. A notice assuring mothers that no charge would be made for weighing babies after one o'clock in the afternoon had been preserved in the store archives, together with some weight records.[24] By the mid-1930s, Rendell's hegemony as Auckland's babywear specialists was challenged by neighbouring George Court's who advertised themselves as 'Auckland's leading House for Quality Baby-wear at lower prices'.[25] Among the components of that store's 'Cosy Winter Wardrobe for Baby', was a ten-pence towelling feeder in pink, blue, or white, complete with a map of New Zealand, presumably for those babies with a yet undeveloped sense of geography and nationhood.[26]

The transition from clothing for babies, through children, to that for adults, although clearly defined by its location on different floors within department stores during this period, was progressive and 'seamless'. The menswear, youths' and boys' departments were usually grouped on the ground floor, but the babies', younger children's and maids' clothing departments were often together on a separate floor from the fashion showroom and the adjacent millinery department. Sometimes styles in children's wear mimicked adults' fashions of the time. In 1925, in the same millinery advertisement featuring 'Just ten French models — to clear at 25/- each', the DIC in Dunedin offered hats in the children's department: 'For the tiny tots, Wee Models just like grown-ups. Little Poke, Cloche and Mushroom shapes; Plain and Floral trimmed. Usually 7/11–25/- each, to clear 2/11, 5/11, 9/11 each.'[27] Hats were required formal wear for little girls, as for women. The traditional rite of passage from babyhood to childhood, and thence to the boys' and youths' department or to maidswear, was ordered by gender, and by size according to age in years; it was also marked by the conformist requirements of school uniform.

Department stores vied with each other to provide school clothing for children. Whether these were the distinctive uniforms of the country's private schools, or the generic gym-frocks, shorts and shirts for public schools and colleges, the supply of school outfits was an important sales exercise, and often used department stores' own manufacturing workrooms. Brown, Ewing catered for the elite schools of Dunedin. The DIC in Christchurch offered boys' college suits for St Andrew's, Cathedral Grammar, Christchurch West, Christ's College, and all primary schools, while Armstrong's added St Bede's to their list.[28] Ballantynes' Timaru House branch, like its founding store in Christchurch, had close links with the boarding houses of local secondary schools, supplying Craighead school uniforms among others.[29] George Court's offered to supply 'all boarding needs for all Auckland private and public schools including St Peter's School, Cambridge' and to mark all uniforms with the student's full name, free.[30]

Until the 1950s, much of the secondary school uniform was largely standardised, with navy or grey shorts and shirts for boys, and gym-frocks and blouses for girls. Blazers, pullovers, socks, caps, and panama and felt hats, had special embroidered

A boy being outfitted with a school uniform in a Christchurch department store, possibly the DIC, c.1960. PHOTOGRAPH: F. E. MCGREGOR. 1982.122.7, CANTERBURY MUSEUM.

James Smith's 'Tom Brown school clothes' for boys – suits in 'a style for every school and college' including Wellington College, Scots College and Rongotai College. PA COLLECTION 3332 – 01, ALEXANDER TURNBULL LIBRARY, WELLINGTON.

badges and distinguishing coloured stripes, which stores were geared to produce. The provision of school uniforms was a profitable venture, and mothers found the stores convenient and reliable. Occasionally fathers accompanied sons to buy the necessary shorts and shirts. As a third-former in 1928, Frank Rogers remembered his father introducing him to the managing director of Milne & Choyce, J. S. Milne, who outfitted him with the regulation clothing for Auckland Grammar School. For most children, however, the racks of clothes were of 'uniform' dullness. Additional requirements were also standardised. Girls were decked out in white wrap-around cooking smocks and caps, as well as the requisite gloves for street-wear, woollen stockings, and 'black Italian cloth bloomers'.[31] Boys were outfitted with thick woollen socks, ties and caps. 'If a boy said "That's too heavy, I don't like it, I want something lighter", we would say to them,

94

The ordered ranks of the school uniform department, Milne & Choyce, c.1950.
PHOTOGRAPH: WALTER J. THOMPSON. REAY CLARKE COLLECTION, J. GRANT.

"That is the school uniform, that is what you have to have"', recalled Brian O'Connor, a shop assistant at George Court's. Regulated by educational and parental authority that was reinforced by the stores themselves, school uniforms were hardly the ranges of clothing from which future consumer interest and enthusiasm were likely to develop.[32]

The conformity of school wear was matched, until the 1950s, by the everyday clothing worn by most girls and boys. If school uniforms were boring and uncomfortable, and linked with the discipline and rigours of education, conventional daywear for children gave no particular encouragement to future consumers of department store fashion either. Despite occasional efforts to encourage mothers to instil desire and preference in young children — such as the article 'Children and their Clothes' in the April issue of the *Mirror* of 1927 — their clothing was often selected by mothers in the children's absence.[33]

Recognising that children's clothing might be outgrown before it was worn out, chain stores such as Woolworth's and McKenzie's competed with department stores to offer cheaper leisure clothes. A 1933 Ballantynes newspaper advertisement, 'Holiday wear for the young folk', featured a mother with three children and offered 'Sound values, practical styles and moderate prices'.[34] Some years later, Milne & Choyce's advertisement for small girls' 'smart and sensible holiday garb', stated 'holiday time is a good time to bring the children to town for a clothes-buying expedition'.[35] The purchase of such clothing was not instigated by the children themselves; it was the mother as consumer who was the target of marketing and who brought the children in to be outfitted. A 1945 advertisement for George Court's had a picture of a boy dreaming 'I want to build a boat! — I want to be a flying man! — I want to drive a racing car!' with the accompanying text 'While he's dreaming of his future, George Court's are taking care of his present needs . . . we know he'll need a wartime quota of school clothes . . . Mother knows we have quality and value too.'[36] Women by implication were the shoppers, in knowing alliance with the store, while the 'little man' was busy with action.[37] Clothes for children, though attractive in their own traditional way, were not subject to the vagaries and whims of fashion; they were rarely checked out against the latest styles, or discussed with great interest. Their main virtue lay in being hard-wearing and reasonably priced, their purchase necessary as children grew out of existing garments.

The sale of children's and young people's clothing, like that of adults', was subject to the limiting factors of financial hardship and import restrictions during the years from 1930 until the late 1940s. Some garments were made from scratch at home, with department stores competing with specialist haberdashery stores to sell fabric, patterns and other sewing supplies. Ready-made clothing for children was accepted as an option, and given some stores' close proximity to one another, shoppers could easily compare costs. During the difficult economic times of the 1930s, however, many children wore 'hand-me-downs' or cut-down adult clothing. The creation of boys' shorts, lined with flour-bag calico and fashioned from men's worn-out trousers, was considered an important skill, a rite of passage for many home sewers.

An advertisement for Farmers' 'Unity' sewing machines encouraged the making of 'your own and the children's frocks. This sewing machine will enable you to make the daintiest garments . . . and will save you time and money.'[38] In 1935, George Court's gave home sewers a glimpse of 'do-it-yourself' glamour in association with Hollywood and the cinema:

Little Shirley Temple Mannequins will parade in the Dress Material Department wearing Shirley Temple Frocks, made from Shirley Temple Paper Patterns of this famous little actress' frocks . . . these are exclusive to George Court's who have arranged the following unique presentation: — On Friday, from 2.30–4.30 and 7.30 to 8.45 p.m., six little Shirley Temple Mannequins will parade in these frocks in George Court's dress material department. Also, Auckland's own little Shirley Temple (Joy Rountree, winner of the Auckland "Shirley Temple Double" competition and entrant in the New Zealand Competition) will make a personal appearance. The same little mannequins will appear on the stage in the Civic Theatre at the Saturday and Monday matinees of "Curley Top" — a Shirley Temple picture commencing on Friday. [39]

When import restrictions were imposed soon afterwards, and clothing coupons were introduced during World War II, it was an advantage for mothers to be able to create children's garments, even if the yardage of fabric itself, when available, required coupons as well as money.[40]

Toys, though, might ensure future loyalty even if the provision of clothing did not. An astonishing variety of children's toys were imported by department stores in the first decades of the twentieth century. In November 1928, Milne & Choyce's slogan 'Store of a "Million Choices"', which was successfully promoted by that firm for many years, was proudly reported as having been first used by a young boy named Frank, whose photograph appeared in the advertisement under the heading 'the little son of an esteemed customer'.[41] Having come to Auckland for a doctor's visit, and spent some time in the consulting room, he was reported as saying to his mother 'Don't bother about the Doctor now, Mummie [sic], let's go to "Million Choices". Frank's heart was in Toyland but his innocent play of words upon the firm's name is literally true', the advertisement enthused, then proceeded to proclaim the great variety of Christmas gifts available in store.

In the late nineteenth century, some American stores were recorded as operating 'Toylands' for children on a seasonal basis, with a particular focus on the Christmas festival. Stocks were considerably reduced at other times. But toys soon came to be regarded as a way of attracting children throughout the year. Retailers were advised to let the children play with the toys even at the risk of some breakages occurring, for 'the more you can interest them the more their mommas and pappas will come to you when the buying time comes'.[42] In 1896, and for several years thereafter, the DIC in

Wellington used their furniture room as a temporary home for Santa and his display of toys.[43] Kirkcaldie & Stains advertised that their manchester department had been given over to a display of Christmas toys in 1904.[44] In 1909, Smith & Caughey's announced that 'our dress department has been transformed into a beautiful Toyland'.[45] It is clear, however, that by the mid-1920s, many stores had permanent toy departments. Milne & Choyce's first floor, 'remodelled and perfectly appointed', was largely given over to the needs of young people and children, their clothing and toys.[46]

Advertisements for toys, directed at children and their parents, appeared in newspapers during the weeks immediately before Christmas, but stocks for this buying season were built up well in advance. Farmers' issued a supplementary booklet with their October 1923 catalogue, featuring a two-page advertisement directed at children for 'a big Airship Balloon FREE to those who order £1 or more worth of any goods. The biggest balloon you ever saw . . . nearly 24 inches long by 10 inches deep. Remember, the coupon must be sent, or we will not know that there are children in your home. Ask mother to write her order NOW, and so help to make our Buy-in-November Campaign a great success.'[47] The *Dry Goods Reporter*'s suggestion of allowing children to see what they wanted and then to 'torment their parents to the limit' could be exercised at a long distance by mail order just as effectively as in the toy department.

The Depression took its toll on sales in toy departments. As early as Christmas 1929, a note of disquiet can be detected in Kirkcaldie & Stains' advertisement: 'Tomorrow [Christmas Eve] the balance of our huge stock of toys is to be cleared at half price. Give the kiddies plenty of toys this Xmas — it won't cost much at these prices.'[48] One newspaper in early December 1932 stated that 'the shopkeepers have reduced all toy prices from 30 to 50 per cent, as compared with those ruling at this time last year'.[49] On Christmas Eve in that same year, Farmers' in Cashel Street, Christchurch, advertised a Saturday morning auction sale to clear out their entire stock of toys.[50] Just the day before, Hay's had announced that the five dolls' houses displayed in 'Santaville' had been reduced in price. 'They have been made by an unemployed carpenter, and Hay's are helping him sell them.'[51] How many little girls in Christchurch might have dreamed of owning such a dolls' house, yet the unbridgeable gap between 'needs' and 'wants', between hopes and their fulfilment in the heart of the Depression, was clearly expressed in this small advertisement.

It was with some pleasure then, that, after the lean years of the Depression, Farmers' announced in 1937 'our buyers have spared no effort to collect a marvellous array of seasonable goods — ransacked from the four corners of the world . . . . We have recently opened the biggest brightest and most attractive Toy Department in Auckland — crammed with wonderful toys for Girls and Boys of all ages.'[52] George Court's urged adults to 'Bring the Kiddies to "Alice in Wonderland", Admission 3d, On the third floor . . . Father Christmas will be there with a cheery word and a free balloon for every child . . . . and Toys, too. Toys galore on the Third Floor . . . Balls, Books, Dolls and soft, cuddly Animals, besides a host of Cars, Carts and Mechanical Toys to delight the heart of any boy. *It is advisable to inspect early.*'[53] Toy departments piled high with the latest exciting novelties were again beginning to flourish.

Alas, it was only a short time before the imposition of Labour's import restrictions, together with the outbreak of World War II, limited the supply of toys available for department stores. Farmers' toy catalogue lamented 'dolls are scarce this year!! The import restrictions have cut down our supplies considerably and we are unable to feature the excellent assortment we previously had.'[54] By 1942, dolls representing nurses, sailors and soldiers, and a wooden replica of HMS *Achilles*, together with games such as 'Let's build our own fort without cutting or glueing', brought the theatre of war into the toy department.[55] Dolls were locally made with composition heads and fabric bodies. Wooden toys manufactured in New Zealand — fire engines, tip trucks, and prams, pull-along trains and wheel-barrows — predominated. By 1944, toys were miserably few and the brief catalogue was produced on poor quality newsprint.[56] In that same year 'something serviceable' in the way of Christmas gifts was suggested by Farmers': 'Give the youngsters a new bullock-hide School Bag. 21/6. It will last him right through school and college.'[57] Times were tough for children as for adults.

The dwindling toy department in Kirkcaldie & Stains disappeared completely and did not reopen until 1952.[58] By November 1945, however, George Court's were positive and intentional in their advertising: 'Opening tomorrow — Toytown . . . A wonderful, wonderful place filled with hundreds of things to make little folk bright-eyed on Christmas morn. We have hunted high and low for toys this year to be certain of giving them a real never to be forgotten old-fashioned Christmas . . . and collected all the magical things they have dreamed about'.[59] Five years later it was confidently stated 'we're into the land of plenty again' with 'a starry-eyed land that will make little folk rub their eyes in amazement . . . they'll see Jack in the Giant's magnificent castle filled with hundreds of the most heart-delighting toys you've seen in years . . . and dear old Santa is there of course. Have a "Santa photo" taken with him.'[60]

The commercial use of Santa Claus as an iconic figure, claimed by American department stores for his association with the enormous sale of toys at Christmas, dates from the mid-1890s. Before that time, Santa had been largely confined to the domestic setting of home and hearth.[61] Initially many retailers relegated Santa to small, out-of-the-way sections of stores, but even in the 1880s some stores were installing Santa in more prominent locations. In December 1888, Roberts' store in London attracted customers to a decorated Christmas grotto complete with Santa Claus and Cinderella. The *Draper's Record* was enthusiastic about Roberts' Christmas innovation, especially as a reported 17,000 children visited Santa.[62] The Santa grotto was so successful that the idea was promptly copied throughout Britain the following year.[63]

Despite a dour 1892 Christmas Eve editorial in the *Otago Daily Times*, which railed at 'the decking of shops as well as churches and houses with evergreens at Christmas — a custom which sprang from a period far anterior to the revelation of Christianity and is assumed . . . to be derived from the custom prevalent during the Saturnalia of the inhabitants of Rome . . . [which] has fallen almost entirely out of use in our midst', New Zealand department stores were soon to follow overseas trends, decorating their stores and introducing Father Christmas a.k.a. Santa Claus. With an entrepreneurial vision of Christmas to the fore, despite its Jewish heritage, the DIC took the lead. The Wellington DIC, not its main store in frosty Dunedin, announced Santa's advent. Santa, complete with Christmas tree and toys, arrived to take his place among the furniture in Wellington's DIC department store in 1894.[64] His first Dunedin appearance did not take place until 1902, when he and 'his enormous Christmas tree' appeared in the DIC's toy room.[65] In Auckland, his earliest arrival in a city store is recorded in 1903, with his 'headquarters' in the setting of a 'Magic Cave', designed by 'Mr Frank L. Carr Jnr, the celebrated American Decorator' for the DSC (later John Court Ltd). Admission to the magic cave was free.[66] This innovation was a great success and was repeated by the company, and by many other stores in subsequent years. In 1905 George & Kersley Ltd's store 'The Economic' (which merged with Wellington's DIC in 1920) announced in the *Evening Post* that Mother & Father Christmas would arrive by train at the railway station.[67] In 1906, a more elaborate itinerary for the busy couple included calling at Petone and the Hutt, while Punch, an addition to their retinue, travelled in a car from Seatoun, through Miramar, Kilbirnie and Island Bay, even visiting Wellington Hospital on his way to the store in Lambton Quay. In 1912, the first Santa parade in Auckland was organised by Morris's of Karangahape Road. Father Christmas, accompanied by

The southern side of Karangahape Road in February 1928, showing the 1YA radio masts at each end of George Court's roof. Traffic is being directed around the intersection with Queen Street. Rendell's building can be seen above the tram. 4-2365, SPECIAL COLLECTIONS, AUCKLAND CITY LIBRARIES.

three car loads of children, travelled from the railway station in a 'Grand Procession' up Queen Street, Wellesley Street, Symonds Street, Newton Road, Karangahape Road, and so to Morris's store.[68]

Santa's presence was well established as an annual institution in the toy section of New Zealand department stores by the 1920s, the period when the commercialisation of Santa reached its most impressive heights in America.[69] By 1922, Kirkcaldie & Stains were advertising that Father Christmas would meet children in his log cabin — 'a reproduction of the great attraction featured by a London Store last Christmas, and which proved to be the greatest draw they had ever known'.[70] By 1925, Father Christmas was ensconced in Neptune's cave at Kirkcaldie & Stains with a 'Spanish treasure galley and the diver who has discovered the beautiful pearls but has to fight the big Octopus to get them. Every visitor receives a splendid present.'[71] Department stores were each making a special Christmas effort to draw children and parents through their doors, and to encourage them as customers. These years featured relatively low-key attractions, often the ubiquitous magic caves, with bran-tubs and fishing-ponds supplying small

Adults and children greet Santa Claus and a polar bear as they arrive at Armstrong's on a float at Christmas 1929. IMG0054, CHRISTCHURCH CITY LIBRARY.

gifts; but inter-store competition intensified as the gloom of Depression conditions settled over the country. The Christmas toy bonanza and entertainment for children was beginning to incorporate the latest trends in modern technology as department stores desperately sought to maintain seasonal profits.

By 1929, George Court's Santa was presented as the epitome of modernity, with an advertisement portraying him calling children with a radio microphone (for over three years, the 1YA radio station had been broadcasting from that same store building).[72] Despite Santa's use of that modern medium, he also employed traditional trappings, announcing that 'white horses will pull my carriage along the street to George Court's store, my home. Wonderful fairies will be all around.'[73] In coping with modernity and the challenging world of the new, the acknowledgement of traditions from the past could be reassuring.[74] The DIC had Santa Claus introducing Robinson Crusoe to 'the little folk of Christchurch' in 1929, while a few days later and a few blocks away to the

A young girl seems caught up in the magic of solo flight, as she rides in the aeroplane roundabout on Farmers' roof-top playground. 2796, AUCKLAND WAR MEMORIAL MUSEUM LIBRARY.

north, ever-versatile Santa was performing 'thrilling stunts' on a tight-rope on the roof of Hay's new store.[75] Armstrong's invited adults to 'bring the kiddies to meet Santa Claus and the Polar Bear'.[76] In the same newspaper Admiral Richard Byrd's triumphant encircling of the South Pole in his aeroplane *Floyd Bennett* was reported. The great public interest in Byrd's first flight over the North Pole in 1926, and his subsequent explorations of Antarctica in 1929 and 1933–34 with the combination of modern exploration and the lure of the polar regions, was a recurring diversion for children and adults alike through the years of the Depression. Charles Edward Kingsford Smith's record-breaking flight around Australia in 1927, and his crossing of the Tasman Sea from Sydney to Christchurch in 1928 also spurred interest in modern air travel. In store, children's entertainment was beginning to reflect significant change.

By 1930, most of the stores had Santa Claus installed well before Christmas, in company with a sometimes bizarre entourage.[77] At Milne & Choyce's 'Treasure Trove',

'Father Christmas shares John Silver's popularity' and in 1931, George Court's Santa arrived 'with his fairy attendants in his gay carnival carriage — Alice in Wonderland and her husband and children will also be with him'.[78] By 1933, however, the pace was stepping up, as the Depression continued to cast its long shadow over consumers and retailers alike. The DIC's Christchurch store had Santa opening a magic cave: 'You will see Admiral Birdie's [sic] expedition to the Pole, Captain Harry Dadums and Tubby the Penguin will be there as well as the Admiral . . . Ice Grottoes, Polar Bears, Seals and Snowstorms, and the good ship *The Bear of Auckland* ploughing her way through the packed ice-floes'.[79] In a frenzy of entrepreneurial activity, Robert Laidlaw of Farmers' created a Christmas spectacular in Auckland to rival all other department stores in the country. Building a 'Flight to the Great Polar Cave' on the ground floor of his store, he brought Santa Claus by plane to Victoria Park, to be welcomed by crowds of children. From there Santa was driven to Hobson Street to take his place in the grotto of the Silver Princess.[80] Farmers' offered children free flights to Hamilton and back, as prizes for the two sections of an essay competition.[81] Rivalry with Milne & Choyce, who that year had launched their Christmas attraction with a 'Trip to the North Pole in the Flying Bluebird', and George Court's, who claimed that 'Auckland's oldest and most beloved Father Christmas arrives at Karangahape Road on Friday next', was gathering momentum.[82] In 1934 Blythe's in Napier featured: 'Byrd's trip to the South Pole . . . see the life-size Polar Bears, Penguins, Arora [sic] Australis, Byrd's Boat — all moving' as their children's Christmas holiday attraction.[83]

The impression of a trip on a mock aircraft, which had offered children and 'grown-ups who, after all are still boys and girls at heart', a journey to the North Pole, exploited 'the roar of the engine . . . clouds scudding past — the landing on the airfield — bears, walruses, penguins, Eskimos — the Aurora Borealis'. Technology, developed in the nineteenth century to create an illusion of voyaging to far-off places, was being reworked and updated to provide modern entertainment for children at a time of general hardship. The DIC in Christchurch offered a 'lovely land of tropical palm trees, blue skies and Magic Caves' from which children could go for 'a flight in the "Red Comet" aeroplane. They will sail through the clouds and see all sorts of wonderful sights on the flight from England to Melbourne and the most thrilling sight of all is the working model of the Sydney Harbour bridge.'[84] In vying to outdo each other's efforts, and attract children and their parents as customers, major stores attempted ever more ambitious schemes.

Water features competed with ice and snow. Milne & Choyce's 'Trip in the Submarine' in 1932 gave the illusion of underwater travel. The submarine was on-sold to Kirkcaldie & Stains, as they re-focused on catering for children and young people.[85] In striving to outdo Farmers' in 1934, however, Milne & Choyce actually flooded part of their basement area to create an unforgettable water-feature named the 'Lost Canal' upon which real boats transported parents and children around the world.[86] 'On your journey you pass the sacred lake guarded night and day by that queer old dragon "Katore" . . . the Fairy Grotto . . . the flaming mountain, called forth by the magic of "Mahuika" the Goddess of Fire — and a prehistoric camp on the river bank where ancient peoples are cooking their meal and the weird creatures which frequent the river, still roaming in their jungle haunts . . . at the end of the journey those quaint Maori Pixies "Tee Wee" and "Tai Hou" have a present for everyone.'[87] Bryan Boon, now in his seventies, still recalls this attraction with wonder and great pleasure.[88]

Competition was at its most intense in Auckland. Hundreds attended George Court's 1934 parade 'to welcome Auckland's Oldest and Most Beloved Father Christmas when he arrives . . . to open "Wonderland" with Mickey and Minnie Mouse, the Fairies, funny old Ma and Pa Coney, and all our old friends'. The following day, Saturday, 24 November, Robert Laidlaw staged Farmers' first grand parade.[89] Several decorated horse and carts left the store accompanied by 'Waggles and Goggles, The Fat Boy, The Man that Walks on his Hands, Harold Lloyd, the Giant and the Big Fiddle'. Travelling up Pitt Street and into Karangahape Road, past their rival, George Court's, down Queen Street and back up to Hobson Street, Farmers' Santa took up residence in the 'Waitomo Caves' with the spectacle of the 'Organ Loft, Blanket Chamber, King Edward's Court, Bride's Jewels, Crystal Palace, Bridal Cake and Glow-worm Grotto'.[90] The admission price included a gift, and the attraction was advertised as appealing to adults and children alike. By exploiting the advances of modernity, without the undue expense and discomfort associated with travel, Farmers' gave many who would never make the trip to Waitomo, but who could afford the 6d admission fee, the novel illusion of visiting the caves. In contrast to the excitement and excesses of 1934 Auckland, no children's Christmas attractions at all were advertised that year in Dunedin, and there was no sign of Santa in any of that city's department stores. Christchurch, however, had Father Christmas arriving by plane and being escorted from the airport to the DIC flanked by outriders from the Canterbury Riding School.[91] A newborn baby monkey added to the attractions at Hay's roof-top 'Joyland'.[92] One department store in

An interested crowd greet Father Christmas outside the Wyndham Street frontage of the store, in one of the earliest Farmers' Santa parades, 1933 or 1934. The canopy over the main corner entrance is visible (left) with the Hobson Street tram rails in the foreground. Santa sits behind the driver on the horse-drawn float. Note the two boys with their swimming togs under their arms (centre) who may have come from the nearby Tepid Baths. 929, AUCKLAND WAR MEMORIAL MUSEUM LIBRARY.

Christchurch stated its belief that: 'It takes such a little to amuse or excite a child, yet with the whole field of untried pleasures before them, it is a wise parent who introduces the simplest of juvenile amusements to them'.[93] Department store efforts were by far outstripping any category of 'simple amusements'.

The next year George Court's Santa Claus proceeded up Queen Street accompanied by the Boop family of giants, while Laidlaw again paraded Santa around the city centre and installed him at 'Mice City' in the Hobson Street store.[94] In 1936 Armstrong's of Christchurch advertised Santa's arrival by 'seaplane' watched by a crowd on the bank of the Avon River. This seemingly dramatic mode of transport however, was in fact a small clinker-built boat, with a plane-like superstructure built for Santa to ride in.[95] No such tame substitute would serve for Farmers' Santa, who, in 1937, arrived by parachute in the Auckland Domain, missing the Wintergarden glasshouse by inches, and landed in the lily pond before travelling in procession to Farmers' store.[96]

World War II, however, put an end to these escalating efforts to outdo each other, with parades of the departing armed forces replacing the celebration of Santa's arrival. Department store Christmas attractions were conducted on a much more restricted scale, if at all, throughout the war. Many department store basements, the usual sites of magic caves and other delights, were converted to air-raid shelters for staff and public.[97]

Limited as immediate post-war efforts were, they could still be spellbinding. One woman remembers a life-size model of Snow White in a glass case in Farmers' magic cave at Christmas 1945; she was in a deep sleep after being poisoned by the Wicked Queen. It was the first attraction to be offered to children after an absence of several years — certainly the first this seven-year-old had ever seen. The effect was dramatic. To a child this was no model; Snow White was beautiful, and alive, for her chest gently rose and fell — she was actually breathing. How on earth did they get Snow White in there? So dazed was the little girl that she returned through the entrance instead of the exit where her mother was waiting, missed her 'bumper gift for all' and inadvertently launched a 'lost child' search through the store.[98]

In post-war Christchurch James Hay instituted an annual Christmas pageant created by Hay's display staff, comprising floats depicting nursery rhymes and seasonal themes, inspired by John Martin's parade in Adelaide.[99] That same year, 1948, saw Farmers' Santa parade in Auckland successfully reinstated after a long interval. It finished with a convoy of buses carrying 250 children from Auckland orphanages. They were greeted by Santa when they reached the store, and given a two-shilling gift, followed

TOP: New Zealand Territorial Force, Countess of Ranfurly's Own Regiment with Second Lieutenant William G. Caughey leading the platoon in Queen Street, 1940. Private A. W. P. (Bert) Taplin, middle of first row. N. AND B. TAPLIN.

BOTTOM: Father Christmas arrives at Farmers' in one of the first post-war Santa parades. A line of children is being ushered past the crowd and towards the entrance to the store – presumably the children from the children's homes and orphanages who have accompanied the parade in buses and who will meet Santa in the store. 1161, AUCKLAND WAR MEMORIAL MUSEUM LIBRARY.

by refreshments in the tearoom. The following year's planning took into account improvements to the arrangements for the parade: 'Santa's float should be behind floats and in front of orphans. Macy's of New York always have Santa at the end of their procession — there is a build-up of excitement, also it is organisationally easier when reaching the store.'[100]

In those informal planning notes, Farmers' also argued that orphans should continue to feature in their reinstated parade, since their plight was guaranteed to rouse public sympathy. The reasons included being first in setting the example of the 'Spirit of Christmas', 'taking the flavour of advertising from the stunt . . . by having the unfortunate to participate', as a 'gesture by Farmers' to build goodwill, being apparent to the many thousands of adults who witnessed the procession and it was definitely noticed by our customers in the tearooms last year', 'having used the orphans for publicity — it would be noticeable if we dropped them' and that 'the newspapers, who will not tolerate advertising in their own columns, will have a let out in the personal angle'.[101] This does not appear to have been an exercise in altruism, but rather an advertising angle. There was no assumption that the orphans might well be potential, future customers, whose youthful loyalty to Farmers' might be enhanced by such an experience. In contrast to this somewhat exploitive attitude to the children, most department stores in New Zealand, including Farmers' and Milne & Choyce, made donations to local orphanage appeals. At Christmas 1913 the first Methodist Orphanage in New Zealand was opened in Mt Albert, the gift of A. C. Caughey and his sister Marianne Smith.[102] James Hay was closely associated with the work of the Christchurch Combined Orphanages appeal, being its chairman for 25 years, and the facilities of his department store were used for a radio appeal and collection point.[103] In the late 1950s, an anonymous donor funded a day in town for a group of Dunedin orphans which included, among other delights, £2 to spend in Arthur Barnett's department store, followed by afternoon tea at the store tearooms.[104]

While Farmers' went from strength to strength with their Santa parade, they and other New Zealand department stores found it increasingly difficult to maintain interesting holiday features to attract parents and children. In 1951, on the first floor, George Court's displayed 'the only Olympia Sailplane in New Zealand . . . This glider with a wing span of 50ft recently established New Zealand records by flying 65 miles and reaching a height of 8000ft. For the first time in New Zealand you will see a full-sized sail-plane in a Department Store. See this special free attraction for all.'[105] This innovative exhibit recalled Harry Selfridge's coup of displaying Bleriot's famous plane in his Oxford Street store the day after the record flight. But George Court's did not draw the same crowds as Selfridges had.[106] Three years later, George Court's sales manager blamed the weather for poor attendances at 'Lilliput', their May school-holiday attraction staged by Pixietown, which he thought the best yet produced. Despite its colourful and animated small wooden pixies 'attending to all manner of activities and pranks . . . driven from underneath the platform by a maze of shafts, pullies and belts', the general manager had no such illusions: 'It does appear that after three showings, Pixietown no longer attracts children or adults in sufficient numbers to justify retaining it for Xmas. We are exploring all other avenues to find a suitable attraction.'[107] The first showing of 'Pixietown', which had been created by New Zealander Freddie Jones, was in Farmers' in Auckland in the 1930s, and was visited by over 6000 people in one day. So successful was the second generation of 'Pixietowns' that units were manufactured in Nelson and sent to Australia, USA and England where they toured the country for several years.[108]

Despite George Court's general manager's disillusionment, James Smith's Wellington store was still featuring 'Pixietown' as a Christmas drawcard in 1959. Their version of hundreds of little mechanical pixies working and playing was advertised as 'direct from England and Australia'.[109] Their windows, which for many years provided one of Wellington's Christmas attractions, featured more than 350 feet of model railway track through 'Snowville, Cactus Canyon and Bluewater Harbour', the trains being sourced from the Lionel Corporation in New York.[110] In the same season, Palmerston North's Collinson & Cunningham Ltd, established in 1904, was advertising its underground fairyland in the basement.[111] This large display of miniature working figures continued to be maintained and reworked for many years after the store was taken over by Farmers', ultimately becoming a 'retro' icon of a vanished form of children's entertainment.

Easter could also offer an opportunity to draw children into the stores. The novelty of 'Hetty the Hen', who laid chocolate eggs to the accompaniment of loud and triumphant clucking, was 'well received by the customers if not by the staff in the near vicinity', reported George Court's sales manager in 1954, and added 'the fact that 11,457 persons bought an Easter Egg each' proved its popularity.[112] 'Hetty the Hen' contained a woman staff member who knitted to while away the time, and discreetly rolled chocolate eggs down a chute at the front of Hetty while monitoring

Looking down Broadway, Palmerston North, c.1937, with Collinson & Cunninghame's department store, later Farmers'(left). ST 90, PALMERSTON NORTH CITY LIBRARY PHOTOGRAPHIC COLLECTION.

the sound recording. The merchandising manager estimated that, without Hetty, only 400–500 of the threepenny Easter eggs would have sold. The sales success was an incentive to repeat the feature, 'although another situation further away from the door would be better', presumably taking customers into the heart of the shop and past more merchandise.[113] One Farmers' staff member, Bryan Burton, recalled that in the Bazaar department (later called the Thrift department), during one school holiday, 'what appeared to be the first essay in automation appeared in the form of a large grey elephant. When a child dropped a threepence into a slot, a bag of sweets was ejected from the trunk. It was years later . . . that I met a staffer . . . who had been crouching inside the animal and manually supplying the goods. The department should have been called "The Bizarre".' At times, very successful holiday drawcards were staged. In August 1953 Cole's Circus occupied the Farmers' parking area and provided a profit for charity.[114] By February 1958, a very successful London Wax Works show during the summer holidays made a profit of £300.[115]

Circuses and waxworks, successful as they may have been, were traditional attractions, but department stores were also moving into the provision of more modern ventures. The space age was under way. A series of artificial earth-satellites had been launched by the Soviet Union, beginning in October 1957 and had caused much interest in the night sky. In 1959, Kirkcaldie & Stains' Christmas attraction was a 'Futuristic Satellite'. This working model had first been shown at Farnborough, and had then been on view at the static exhibition that marked the opening of Wellington's airport in November 1959. It was 'in action from 10am to 2pm daily on the hour'.[116] In 1958 Farmers' was looking forward to the celebration of its jubilee year, and was considering equipping a planetarium for the city, at a cost of approximately £4000, to mark the occasion. Robert Laidlaw would have preferred the planetarium to have been installed in Farmers' own buildings, but by agreement the Auckland War Memorial Museum was chosen as the site of that department store sponsorship of up-to-the-minute interest in outer space. Not only was the amenity set up, it was hoped that with an ongoing contribution of £750 from Farmers' each year for three years, the museum authorities would be able to make admission free for that period.[117]

Department stores constantly searched for the novelties to entice potential customers, whether it was Hector the parrot's birthday at Farmers' or exploiting the growing interest in anthropological studies, with a focus on Maori story-telling tradition. Milne & Choyce's Christmas feature in 1927 had an unusual cultural dimension:

> Now Listen Children! Rangi the famous Rotorua Guide arrives one day next week (Thursday to be exact) bringing a friend with her and they will make the Milne & Choyce Store their home for a few days. They are coming specially to be amongst the children — to tell those quaint Maori stories and legends that are so interesting to anyone between the ages of 4 and 74. Guide Rangi will be on the first floor and when you have parties in the 'Tudor' Room, she will be there. Guide Rangi is a delightful hostess, and you simply must meet her.[118]

The offering of department store tearooms as venues for such children's parties, whether at Christmas or during the year, featured in advertisements.[119] In December 1929, the Christchurch DIC publicised 'another Golliwog Tea next Saturday 10.30–11.30, tickets 1/-'.[120] Soon after opening, George Court's announced that 'children's

The clock has struck twelve in this elaborately detailed window display, one of a series of scenes from Milne & Choyce's Christmas presentation of *Cinderella*, which children and adults alike enjoyed in the post-war years. 90.1.49, AUCKLAND WAR MEMORIAL MUSEUM LIBRARY.

parties [were] especially catered for every Saturday morning in the new Tearoom, "Overlooking Auckland".[121] By 1939, when World War II had begun, a specially planned tea party was to be held on Saturday morning by 'The Wizard of Oz', assisted by 'Neddo'. 'Your last opportunity to book for the grand tea party to be held by the Wizard of Oz in George Court's Tearooms on Saturday December 9th. Come and meet the Scarecrow, The Cowardly Lion and the Tin Woodman. Win a double free Pass to the Embassy Theatre! Lots of lovely things to eat — Tickets 1/-.'[122]

The varied attractions that the children's floors of department stores offered made them places where expectations of excitement and variety ran high. Outside the stores, in window displays, on roof-top playgrounds or in the main streets of towns and cities their imaginative and innovative activities and parades linked department stores in children's minds with those memorable presentations. It is significant that Mavis Jaggar-

Smith's pleasurable memories of her family's visits to department stores with which this chapter began, are not of the buying of goods — clothing or toys — but rather are associated with the special services Farmers' offered its visitors to the roof-top area. The children's playground, the fascination of the redoubtable Hector, and the tearoom as the place for rest and refreshment, were all linked together in a happy blend of action, wonder and satisfaction.

Many people recall the department store tearooms and the food they enjoyed there as one of the great joys of their childhood. Up at the top of the store, with echoes of those familiar fairy stories, they could choose whatever they wished from the menu, and it would be brought to them. In 1959, James Smith's was advertising a tearoom special of 'quaint little Pixieland cakes . . . to delight any youngster'. (Any doubts that mother as consumer might have had about the origin of such cakes were immediately dispelled by the note, 'made in our own kitchen'.)[123] After a morning of shopping with mother, experiencing the colour, bustle and new sights to be seen in the stores, tired, hungry and helping to carry some of the accumulation of packages, it is time to enter the crowded lift again for the short trip upwards to the tearooms and some of those delicious fairy cakes.

CHAPTER FOUR

Top Floor — Tearooms: Going Down

> We [Geoffrey de Montalk and Maxwell Rudd] were in the habit of having lunch together in the restaurant at the top of Milne and Choyce's sky-scraper in Queen Street . . . When I got round to meeting R. A. K. Mason who surely was a genuinely significant poet though a rabid Communist, he, Maxwell Rudd and I . . . used to foregather for lunch in Milne and Choyce's above mentioned upper-middle-class restaurant on the top floor of their upper-middle-class skyscraper and there we had great discussions as to how you scan English poetry. It is quite obvious that nobody has solved this problem.[1]

Geoffrey de Montalk saw himself at the centre of a group of young men about town, engaged with important, weighty literary debate in Milne & Choyce's newly opened Tudor Room. For that select circle who 'believed themselves to be a poetic aristocracy through which the now decadent traditions of English poetry would be revitalised', this was a fashionable meeting place where Geoffrey's presence, especially if engaged in opinionated and vociferous discussion, might well be noticed.[2] The flamboyant and aspiring poet would probably not have glanced at the other diners around him as he held forth above the murmur of conversation, but the Tudor Room was usually crowded. Business men exchanged the latest prices from the share-market over a mixed grill. A mother and daughter, intent on buying wedding outfits and trousseau linen, animatedly compared the white lace and silk on offer at Smith & Caughey's with that on display in Milne & Choyce, as they daintily ate their salmon mayonnaise. Two children on their best behaviour looked with awe as ice-cream sundaes were placed before them; such special treats were rare when most homes did not possess refrigerators. The tearoom manager, stately in her long frock, corsage pinned to her shoulder, sailed serenely down the carpeted aisles of the enormous space, seating men, women and children in cosy alcoves with large windows and dark, floral chintz drapes, or at the myriad of tables set in ordered rows. The tablecloths and napkins were starched, crisp and white. The array of silver cutlery gleamed, and a vase of fresh flowers added a charming note to the setting. The appetising smell of roast meat and vegetables, of casseroles and pies and other delicious hot and cold dishes, wafted through the tearoom. An attentive waitress in cap and frilly apron immediately appeared, pencil and pad in hand to take orders. It was a busy lunch-time at the heart of 1925 Auckland.

Queen Street, Auckland, with the Bank of New Zealand building (extreme right) and Milne & Choyce's building (second from right) before the further four floors were added in the early 1920s. The trams have pride of place with few motor cars in sight. 046203, ALEXANDER TURNBULL LIBRARY, WELLINGTON.

The recently opened Tudor Room on the seventh floor of Milne & Choyce. Diners could also be seated at the windowed alcoves on both sides of the large space. *WHEN YOU ARE IN AUCKLAND: MILNE & CHOYCE LTD.: BETWEEN THE BANKS: QUEEN STREET, AUCKLAND N.Z.* [C.1924–26].

In step with the tempo of the twentieth century, a buoyant Milne & Choyce was on the up and up. The firm first leased, then bought, a three-storey wooden property in Queen Street, between Wyndham and Swanson Streets, in 1909. With a spectacular increase in business turnover by 1921, a massive enlargement of these premises into the seven-storey 'skyscraper' was begun by Fletcher Construction Company, in association with architect Lew Piper. When planning for their smart new building, Milne & Choyce hoped to create an up-market restaurant, which would 'cater principally for morning and afternoon teas with a midday light luncheon service'.[3] A vast, wood-panelled tearoom and an adjoining roof-garden were the new building's topmost features when it was completed in 1924. The tearoom's chosen name, the 'Tudor Room', with its historical and literary associations, was already in use at Beath's department store in Christchurch. The name reassured patrons that, although these were the latest, largest, and most modern eating-places in the city, traditional values and standards were also being honoured. Affirming colonial links with English imperial heritage and suggesting the wealth of an era where grandeur of scale and regal extravagance in the provision of food was legendary, the name conferred dignity and status on those who ate there.[4]

Surprisingly, in the recent feast of writing about department store culture and consumption food services have been neglected. Yet the role of the tearoom, as a place where the eating of food was both discreet and conspicuous, embodies consumption in its most overt form. By travelling to the top floor of these department stores, we can venture into the crowded tearooms and savour a vanished world. Among the potted palms and tiered, silver cake-stands, above the buzz of conversation, we can hear the gentle clink of silver tea service, the clatter of cutlery upon monogrammed china, and the drift of music from piano or string trio.

Kirkcaldie & Stains had opened a tearoom in their new, four-storey brick building in Lambton Quay on 7 July 1898.[5] Within a few months, this popular meeting place achieved widespread publicity thanks to a notorious shooting incident, fortunately not fatal, which involved two women (one the tearoom's manager). The assailant calmly made her way down the staircase, smoking revolver in hand, and was apprehended on the ground floor.[6] An encounter of a very different nature took place in Milne & Choyce's Refreshment Room, when Mavis Jaggar-Smith's mother-in-law, as a very young woman, was having tea with her friend, May Hurley: 'They were both beautiful young ladies and noticed that a young man kept glancing at them and making notes. In a well-bred fashion they pretended to ignore him until he approached their table, bowed low and handed them a pencil sketch of themselves. It was signed by "Goldie".'[7]

What was the recipe for a successful tearoom? Creating the right image was just as important as serving the right food. Management and restaurant staff saw themselves in the vanguard of modernity and hoped to attract patrons by projecting an aura of fashion à la mode. Boasting the latest in up-to-date kitchen equipment, and presenting an array of appetising food in spacious, tasteful settings, a stylish tearoom could be one of the most important amenities offered by a department store. Well positioned to offer diners panoramic views, with electric lifts providing access, a top-floor tearoom proclaimed the cachet of the store's multi-storey construction and the firm's similarly elevated status. It represented a significant expression of technological achievement. An exception, Kirkcaldie & Stains' new tearoom, built just before the turn of the century, was sited on the first floor rather than the highest reaches of the fourth. Since lifts were not installed until the construction of their adjacent ferro-concrete building in 1909, ease of customer access by stairway would have outweighed any consideration of Wellington's views.[8]

When Beath's opened their Tudor Tea Room in 1915, they crowned the dizzy heights of their six-storey building with New Zealand's first roof garden. Large plate-glass windows were set in the building's concrete parapet offering amazing panoramic views far beyond Christchurch itself. Beath's was proudly reckoned to be the tallest drapery store in the Dominion, with every floor reached by the Otis electric lift 'which travelled at 225 feet a minute, and was guaranteed absolutely safe even if the hauling rope broke'.[9] The record was soon challenged, when John Court's sixth floor, roof-top

The roof garden and early tearooms on Beath's department store. 1993.346.1, CANTERBURY MUSEUM.

tearoom opened on 6 December 1916, just in time for the Christmas trade. It was the culmination of an extensive building programme that doubled the size of the existing three-storey structure and reached 'the full height permitted under the City Council by-laws — 100 ft above the level of Queen Street'.[10] As well as offering male patrons an adjacent smoking lounge, the tearoom presented 'dainty high-grade lunches and morning and afternoon teas'. This dining space was to become a popular feature of the store, with some customers regularly meeting there for over half a century.[11] With a capacity to seat 160 people, it was the first of Auckland's large department store tearooms and the first to enjoy extensive city and harbour views.[12]

Three electric lifts brought patrons and supplies to John Court's tearoom.[13] Its publicity promoted a modern and healthy kitchen 'where practically everything is done by means of mechanical or electrical devices. Constant handling is thus diminished.'[14] Equipment included a bread-cutting machine and an 'electric dish-washer which handles thousands of pieces of china every day with scarcely a casualty'.[15] Eight years

John Court's roof garden on a sunny day, c.1922. *THE CITY OF ENTERPRISE.*

later, shortly before the opening of Milne & Choyce's Tudor Room, a 'mechanical force fresh air supply system of ventilation was installed in the Tea Room and Kitchen'.[16] In 1928 it was estimated that a refrigerator, newly purchased for the Tudor Room, would effect a saving of £60 a year on ice-cream alone, and reduce wastage on other foodstuffs to a minimum.[17]

The kitchen's efficiency, however, did not intrude upon the calm and attractive atmosphere of John Court's tearoom itself. Bowls of pink sweetpeas and curtains of shadowed chintz complemented a subdued colour scheme of fawn and grey.[18] Exotic variety was displayed in the adjoining roof garden where 'a collection of interesting plants, living birds, gaily plumaged, and quaint fishes' could be observed and large potted plants included a lemon tree.[19]

In 1917 Blythe's of Napier celebrated the opening of a tearoom on the second floor of the new 'handsome three storied building in ferro-concrete', adjoining their premises in Napier. It could be reached from the ladies' showroom, through the men's departments in Emerson Street or the carpet department in Hastings Street.[20] This elegant tearoom, with its walls panelled in ash and framed in Oregon pine, its cool colour scheme of grey upholstered oak furniture with blue and grey Axminster carpet, was sadly short-lived, becoming a casualty of the 1931 earthquake. Ballantynes' first-floor tearoom in Christchurch also met a tragic fate, being destroyed by fire on 18 November 1947. It was reached through a luxuriously appointed lounge at the head of the grand staircase. Designed by Cecil Wood, and lavishly appointed and decorated, it had opened in 1919 to a tremendous crowd of 2000 (only 500 had been expected).[21]

Vases of daffodils decorate the tables at Ballantynes' tearoom in 1938. A few men and women customers choose seats by the windows to enjoy the spring sunshine. Piles of crisply laundered table napkins can be seen on one table (left foreground). 171MG0054, CHRISTCHURCH CITY LIBRARY.

Two years later, despite difficult economic conditions, Farmers' Trading Company opened a tearoom alongside the children's playground on the roof of its new seven-storey building in Auckland's Hobson Street.[22] This dining venue was not without problems, for high top floors bore the brunt of prevailing wind and rain: 'Every winter we have great difficulty with the water driving through the walls of the Tea Room and discoloring the interior of the walls, and they have frequently to be recalcimined, but in spite of this the walls are in a very unsightly condition as the weather is through again in a few days'. Rather than plastering the outside of the brickwork it was suggested that 'panelling the interior with oak, in keeping with the present work around the Kitchen leaving same 1½ inches away from the wall, and ½ inch up from the floor, so as to leave a free draught of air . . . would contribute to the appearance of the room' and would be less costly.[23] In the 1920s, as today, leaky buildings brought their share of worry,

Farmers' new art deco tearoom, designed by Roy Lippincott and opened in 1930. M. KAY.

inconvenience and extra expense. Robert Laidlaw's free transport strategies, combined with Farmers' massive advertising campaigns, brought an increase in patronage of his store and tearoom. Facilities became inadequate as well as leaky, and it was decided to build a new public dining room on the roof of the adjacent annexe.

Farmers' hall for public dining was lavishly conceived and was influenced by art deco style, with a vaulted ceiling, panoramic windows and stone walls. The services of leading architect Roy Lippincott were used to design the interior of the large space.[24] This 'grandeur on an unprecedented scale' was launched in a blaze of fashion in September 1930, by Lady Orford, with the first mannequin parade of all New Zealand-made attire to be held in the Dominion.[25] So successful was this venture that the programme was extended, and it was estimated that 3600 people viewed the parade in Farmers' new tearoom, which seated 300.[26]

There was already an established pattern of fashion parades being held in Farmers' former tearoom, with an autumn and spring 'Promenade des Modes Parisiennes' during 1927.[27] In the late 1920s, Paris was well established as a symbol of urban modernity; the 1925 Paris Exhibition had been a momentous occurrence, associating that city with the latest in consumption and display. By implication, the style and glamour of Paris was now available to those who patronised department stores such as Farmers', and took refreshments in their tearooms.[28]

The completed DIC store in Wellington. 015024, ALEXANDER TURNBULL LIBRARY, WELLINGTON.

Modern style was important in Wellington's DIC restaurant too. Opened in their new building at the end of February 1929, the novel attraction of New Zealand's first escalator, a drawcard for many years, carried marvelling customers up to the first floor tearoom. This was 'artistically panelled in Queensland Maple [with] unusual fluted columns with bronze caps adding considerably to the dignified and handsome effect'.[29]

Such impressive and spectacular expenditure would soon be curtailed. The 'sugarbag years' of the Great Depression were upon New Zealand. During difficult times from 1933 to 1937 Farmers' operated a cash retail store in the Winstone building in Queen Street, in an effort to reach customers who would not make the trip up to its flagship Hobson Street store; but the Queen Street store made heavy losses. Laidlaw,

New Zealanders out shopping at the DIC, Wellington, 1929. CHRISTOPHER PERKINS,
BY PERMISSION JANE GARRETT. C 064-021, ALEXANDER TURNBULL LIBRARY, WELLINGTON.

ever the shrewd businessman, suggested blocking off its centre door to make the store
look busier at the side entrances and also to keep people from seeing its emptiness from
the big main door: 'This again would help the psychology of the public who naturally
like to trade at a busy shop'. Even in this situation, a tearoom was seen as a necessary
adjunct for shoppers, and one was installed in the basement. With a cup of tea priced at
only one penny, this service managed to make an initial profit.[30]

Four years after Farmers' unprecedented expenditure on a new tearoom for its
Hobson Street site, and almost ten years after Milne & Choyce's Tudor Room had been
established, George Court's, in Karangahape Road, Auckland, built a large, top-floor
tearoom to accommodate 350 people, at a cost of £20,000.[31] Despite greatly depressed
trading conditions, the opening took place on Monday, 21 November 1934, just in time

to cater for Santa's arrival at the store on the Friday of that same week; charges were 'in keeping with the firm's traditional policy of quality at the lowest possible price'.[32] The panoramic views of Auckland city, suburbs and harbour were again represented as drawcards by yet another contender for tearoom patronage, together with 'quiet coolness . . . in hot sultry summer days — as refreshing as an ocean breeze'.

By the mid-1930s, height was no longer considered so important by Beath's management. The roof-top dining space now became the staff café. Following a major reconstruction of the Christchurch store, most of the first floor of the Cashel and Colombo Street block was given over to a stately restaurant with a lofty ceiling, parquet floor and dark green walls, decorated with gold leaf. Opened in 1935, with the famous Christchurch cook, Miss Trent, in charge of the kitchen, this tearoom was reputed to be one of the finest in the country. It could accommodate 600 at one time, and on average 30,000 people availed themselves of its smart service every month, using specially designed fine china, imported from England.[33]

Conventional wisdom maintained that the higher the floor, the less likely it was to be visited by potential customers to the store: 'In view of the fact that about three-fourths of department store customers seldom go above the first floor, the food-serving department stands as a potential business builder if it can draw people above the first floor and into contact with other departments seldom visited otherwise'.[34] For department store managers, the use of a large, remote space for a restaurant could be a winner but it was risky. If the mix of retail goods and food service failed to draw customers up through the multi-levelled stores, the top-floor tearooms could become wasted space.

Early tearooms had featured roof-top gardens as an added attraction. In the 1930s, however, the gardens were beginning to lose their appeal. The novelty was wearing off, and open spaces had demonstrable drawbacks. Milne & Choyce's tearoom balcony, which formed a roof-garden on the Queen Street frontage of the store, met with early problems because of inclement weather and Auckland's prevailing nor'-easterly winds. The City Council declined permission for the store to enclose the area because of the fire risk.[35] A year's negotiation with the council made little headway, but finally the already large Tudor Room became even larger, and the need to maximise use of the tearoom in relation to the store and its customers became even greater. [36]

Amazing numbers of customers made the trip to these top-of-the-store tearooms. In 1934, twenty-one-year-old Gwen Petch (née Hewson) had hoped to take a degree

LEFT: John Court fitted a large number of patrons into their popular sixth-floor tearooms in the late 1930s. G. PETCH. RIGHT: A view of part of Milne & Choyce's Tudor Room, ready for morning or afternoon tea in 1948. A 'Tudor Menu' stands on each table and there are reversible 'customer waiting' signs in holders on top of each silver cake-stand. 4451A, AUCKLAND WAR MEMORIAL MUSEUM LIBRARY.

in Home Science at Otago University, but instead was attending Auckland University College and completing her BA, which included a chemistry paper. She was teaching domestic science part-time at her old school, Auckland Girls' Grammar, when approached by John W. Court to become manager of their tearoom. By the time she left, in 1941, she was earning £6 15s per week, a larger wage than she could have earned as a secondary school teacher. Gwen recalled that a record 4000 people had patronised John Court's restaurant one Friday.[37] Most of them would have taken the lifts to the fifth floor and walked up the stairs to the tearoom on the next floor, with this stairway often accommodating a patient queue of people.

Alongside refreshments, tearooms also provided a prompt and reasonably priced lunch-time service for women and men who worked in the central business district. One Wellington typist who lunched regularly in the 1920s with a friend at Kirkcaldie &

Stains remembered that they were able to enjoy 'ham and tongue, mashed potatoes, a scone and butter and a pot of tea for . . . 9d'.[38] During the 1920s, Farmers' targeted both men and women with their 'light luncheons for Business Men and Girls'. Their Auckland version of 'ham and tongue, with salad, bread and butter, tea or coffee', was a whole sixpence dearer, however, at 1s 3d.[39] When Mary Pilkington worked as a copywriter at Farmers' through the 1940s, she often lunched at Milne & Choyce's tearoom: 'They had special alcoves and people would meet there every day . . . you'd see all kinds of business and professional people from round the town who ate there regularly, and with whom they would dine . . . the tearoom was lovely . . . with very nice things to eat . . . at remarkably small cost, but of course our wages were very low'.[40] Later, when Mary worked at Milne & Choyce with artist Olive Lloyd, they both continued to lunch at the Tudor Room.

Catering for central city workers was a deliberate strategy. It established attitudes of appreciation for well-prepared and promptly served meals in pleasant surroundings, and built up patterns of loyalty to a particular store. Although department stores have generally been seen as places patronised by women, their tearooms were not perceived as just places for ladies to lunch. Many men regularly used department store tearooms and met their friends over a meal. Networking with professional and commercial colleagues was important as towns and cities grew. Tearoom manager Gwen Petch knew exactly where her regular businessmen liked to be seated each lunch-time, and also what they enjoyed eating; such friendly and attentive consideration did not go unnoticed.

A friendly atmosphere included offering appetising food at reasonable prices. During the Depression, Beath's of Christchurch advertised two-course lunches for a shilling.[41] A Ballantynes menu from the early 1930s, however, offered an extensive menu with a minimum charge of 1s 3d; included were oysters on the shell and lobster mayonnaise. The only dishes at 1s 3d were 'Cheshire cheese pie', 'Savoury Shepherd's Pie and Sauce Piquant', a 'single chop', or an 'entree of steak', hot from the grill. Asparagus cream soup (3d) with a dessert of Peach Melba (1s) presented another minimum charge option for those with a sweet tooth.[42] Kirkcaldie & Stains' 1933 menu listed a three-course lunch for 1s 9d, with all menu items available separately. A grill service, stipulating a ten-minute ordering time, indicated that meal service was very prompt. Among the dishes listed were 'Crème of oyster soup', 'Fried filleted flounder & egg sauce', with entrees including 'Steak and kidney pie', 'Crumbed cutlets and tomato sauce', 'Poached egg and spinach' and 'Macaroni cheese'; there were roast and boiled meats, cold joints, vegetables — 'Baked or mashed potatoes and spring cabbage' — and a variety of sweets, hot and cold, with cream or sauce. For the culinary sophisticate there was a selection of olives available (6d) to commence the meal.[43]

By late 1933, the '"Karo" Tea & Luncheon Rooms over Rendells Ltd' had closed and a 'new modern tearoom on the first floor down' opened.[44] By winter 1934, Rendell's had identified economic considerations as most important in its 'most moderate' charges for afternoon teas and lunches. A 'wonderful Two-course luncheon for 1/-, Three-course 1/3' was offered.[45] This price was matched by others. The Vegetarian Café in Queen Street also provided a three-course meal for 1s 3d, with 'salad dishes, and stewed fruits'.[46] Cookes' Restaurant, also in Queen Street, offered affordable prices too in their selection of grills and stated: 'Our trade with these very popular dishes is increasing each day, and we have had to employ extra staff to cope with the increasing volume of business . . . cooked by Women Chefs, with our own special methods, which make these dishes so enticing'.[47] 'Everyone enjoys our Dinners. They're so like the meals that mother cooks.'[48]

By the 1930s, despite the Depression and competition from High Street restaurants, most major department stores offered their customers large and spacious eating-places. H. & J. Smith even boasted a double-sided dining room with two back-to-back fireplaces sending their warmth in each direction, a feature which was particularly cosy on chilly Invercargill days.[49] Establishing and maintaining patterns of usage and commitment required steady promotion. In the early, inter-war era, after prohibition had almost carried the day in the poll of 1919, many people felt a strong antipathy towards hotels seeing them as alien and threatening environments, and refusing to condone the liquor trade by dining in them. By contrast, department store tearooms offered friendly, respectable and smart options for alcohol-free dining. They promoted 'dainty' and light alternatives to the heavy meals traditionally served in hotels and grill-rooms, a midday option that was welcomed by many men as well as women.

Food service brought department stores important publicity. On 19 January 1954, Beath's hosted a civic banquet for 300 guests in the green and gold restaurant, specially decorated with red, white and blue flowers to welcome Her Majesty Queen Elizabeth and the Duke of Edinburgh on their royal tour. The next day, the Duke and 446 guests attended a Canterbury Chamber of Commerce luncheon at the same venue. The Overseas League later greeted 500 guests at yet another function at Beath's, a reception

Royal Tour 1953–54: Her Majesty and His Royal Highness with the Mayor of Christchurch, Mr R. M. McFarlane, M.P., at the civic dinner at Beath's, 19 January 1954. PHOTOGRAPH: MR CHRISTIANSEN. ARCHIVES NEW ZEALAND/TE RUA MAHARA O TE KAWANATANGA WELLINGTON OFFICE. ALEXANDER TURNBULL LIBRARY 42330½ (AAQT 6538 28/C/16)]

for six members of the royal entourage.[50] This was New Zealand department store publicity of the highest order.

There were more subtle ways, however, to attract customers to store premises. A large advertisement aimed at men promoted the importance of preparing for winter health by wearing warm but fashionable clothes. It linked fashion and business success with food by stating 'Quick service and perfect cooking are daily attracting more men to George Court and Sons Ltd's Restaurant and Tearooms, "Overlooking Auckland" Open daily from 9.30 a.m. A Private Room, eminently suitable for business conferences,

Silver milk jug and sugar bowl on their stand, with the George Court crest visible. G. FORTUNE.

etc., is available at a moderate charge.'[51] Business could also be linked with politics. Before the 1935 general election, Sir Heaton Rhodes chaired an early meeting of the National Political Federation, later to evolve into the National Party, in Ballantynes' tearoom.[52] That same firm was the recognised provider of academic and clerical garb for Christchurch. In a pattern established over many years, Ballantynes provided free afternoon tea for Canterbury University College graduates and staff in their proud, capping regalia, after they had marched to the store from the Students' Union building at the old university. Sometimes as many as 200 attended.[53] Whether in recognition of their purchase of robes for graduation, as an exercise in publicity, or an investment in loyalty, this generous gesture affected increasing numbers of women, as well as future business and professional men of Christchurch.

Store tearooms offered a place where the requirements and obligations of hospitality could be catered for with style and grace. These grand public spaces, comfortable and well appointed, offered women the possibility of dining and socialising. As women moved from the seclusion of home into the community, stores offered their facilities to busy women about town. 'Hostesses will be interested in a beautiful Private Room, which is completely separate from George Court's Main Restaurant and ideal for any social or business function. A western aspect assures good afternoon natural lighting and pleasant sunlight. The charges are most reasonable.'[54] Before its horrific 1947 fire, Ballantynes could cater for up to 400 people in their tearooms, for they had several smaller spaces that were available for private functions as well as their main tearoom and Grill Room. Their Pink and Gold Rooms had a separate private entrance in Cashel Street.[55] Department stores also offered their facilities for wedding receptions. Brides and their families could choose to hold the wedding breakfast either in part of the main tearoom, or in a private room.[56]

Some tearoom advertisements were couched in tones that would appeal to customers with time at their disposal. Farmers' offered to cater for card parties, with 'Bridge afternoons in the tearoom — a charming atmosphere of peace and quietness — a dainty afternoon tea served promptly'.[57] Bridge afternoons afforded a popular, fashionable and effortless way for women to raise funds for their favourite charities, while at the same time enjoying themselves.[58] The silver cake-stands with their three-tiered selection of dainty sandwiches, hot savouries, finely sliced fruit or nut loaf, pikelets, scones, and delicious cream cakes, were a characteristic delight on such occasions. John Court's 1939 menu gave a range of prices for afternoon tea from 'The Premier — 6d' to 'The Dainty — 9d' and 'The Supreme — 1/-'. Each was served with 'Ceylon, China or Russian Tea; Coffee, Cocoa or Milk'. Diners were also informed that the John Court tearoom 'devote[d] special attention to Birthday, Bridge, Reception, Farewell and other private parties . . . Terms Moderate'.[59]

The hosting of women's social and philanthropic clubs, and the patronage of their membership was a distinct advantage to department stores. In 1929 Auckland's Lyceum Club leased the sixth floor of Smith & Caughey's new building, and remained there until 1994. During that time the club members, who numbered over 1000, could access their clubrooms by using the lifts, which were sited near the Wellesley Street entrance to the store. Most, however, preferred to walk through the ground floor from the main doors on Queen Street, and many were valued customers.[60] In 1954, the Gore Women's Club lunched with Queen Elizabeth and the Duke of Edinburgh in their club rooms on the second floor of H. & J. Smith's building, specially decorated for the occasion. Thousands subsequently visited the store to experience for themselves the vicarious thrill of treading in the same steps as the Queen. The Christchurch Travel Club held its monthly meetings in the comfortable surroundings of Ballantynes' tearoom.[61] Eunice Chick, a

Royal Tour 1953–54: Her Majesty Queen Elizabeth II arrives for lunch at the Gore
Women's Club rooms. These were on the second floor of H. & J. Smith's department store
building. ARCHIVES NEW ZEALAND/TE RUA MAHARA O TE KAWANATANGA WELLINGTON OFFICE.
ALEXANDER TURNBULL LIBRARY 42122½ (AAQT 6538 37/C/7)

member of the Auckland Travel Club for 55 years, remembered that when she joined, the club met weekly at Milne & Choyce: 'They would set out morning tea for us and we were waited on. Milne's was very elegant. The waitresses wore snappy little clothes like they do in England. We even had our own furniture, a lot of which was donated antiques . . . Going to the Travel Club was a highlight every week.'[62] In 1943 Farmers' paid £500 towards the cost of renovating an adjacent building in Hobson Street; it was agreed that the Happiness Club be granted the use of the space rent-free, the tenancy to be a temporary one.[63] By 1950 the members of the Happiness Club, a social and charitable club for women, were regularly using Farmers' tearoom for their meetings.[64]

Department stores sought to offer special attractions for women during the Depression years and these often used the tearoom setting. In 1932 hundreds of women thronged Ballantynes' grand staircase and stood in queues to experience the fashion wisdom of Lady Chaytor, 'journalist, lecturer, aviatrix, dress-designer, Girl Guide Commissioner and politician', as she 'emphasised the importance of individuality in dress, the wisdom and economy of planning one's own clothes as the Parisians do, instead of buying hap-hazardly [sic] as many English women still persist in doing'.[65] The indefatigable Lady Chaytor, wife of Sir Edmund Chaytor of Durham, had first appeared in her leather flying suit at Dunedin's town hall in a fashion show sponsored by department store Arthur Barnett Ltd, with proceeds donated to the Unemployed Fund.[66] Following her appearances in Christchurch, she travelled to Wellington, giving one show in the Concert Chamber, from which the proceeds were to be donated to the Mayor's Relief Fund, and one at Kirkcaldie & Stains.[67] The unchanging format of each show, with Lady Chaytor deftly removing her flying gear to reveal a charming afternoon outfit, followed by rapid changes of costume, was accompanied by a fashion parade using models from the local department stores. This dazzling guest offered distracting fare for a country in the grip of a depression.

In the years when hair and beauty salons offered their clients conditions of absolute privacy, Miss Kathleen Court, of 'the Kathleen Court Co. famous cosmeticians', gave a discreet 'lecturette' in Blythe's rebuilt Napier tearooms one Friday afternoon in 1934. 'This Demonstration will be of a private nature, as a portion of the Tea Room has been screened off for the purpose.'[68] Clothes and cosmetics, however, were not so obviously to the fore in the Christchurch welcome to famous aviator Jean Batten two years later. The excitement of solo flight by a woman New Zealand claimed as its own provided a special drawcard at Ballantynes' tearoom.[69]

The orchestra dais in Beath's tearoom. This was situated between the entrances to the dining room and the kitchen. The ceiling of the dining room was white, the walls veridian green with gold mouldings and panel detail, the floors parquet, the grilles bronze. HENDRY COLLECTION. 1985.106.11, CANTERBURY MUSEUM.

In 1933, John Court, 'at the corner' of Queen and Victoria Streets, was promoting its tearoom's musical offerings as well as its reasonably priced food, strengthening its popularity as a meeting place. Advertisements announced that a trio of accomplished musicians played daily while a 'pot of tea of John Court Ltds' own delicious quality, a cup of coffee or of cocoa, or a glass of milk, hot or cold with assorted biscuits' could be had for fourpence.[70] The musicians' repertoire varied from selections from grand opera, to those from light operas by Noel Coward and Ivor Novello.[71] Milne & Choyce also provided musical interludes in their tearooms throughout the years, and in 1934 offered the musically modern their last opportunity of hearing the famous 'Tom Katz Saxophone Band' before they departed 'to fulfil an important London engagement'.[72]

Farmers' had a changing programme of light music every afternoon, Monday to Friday, from 2.30 to 4.30 p.m., with Miss Louise Engel (piano), Mr Henry Engel (violin), and Mr Edward Engel (cello).[73] An impressive quartet of harp, cello, violin and piano brought music to Ballantynes' Christchurch tearoom.[74] Frank Crowther, a gifted musician, was employed by Kirkcaldie & Stains in the 1930s and continued to play the Steinway in their tearoom for 20 years. He was a very popular pianist with an astonishing repertoire, who could respond to an impromptu situation with the appropriate choice of refrain. 'One afternoon', recorded Julia Millen, 'my mother and a friend (both wearing blue) walked to their table to the strains of "Two Little Girls in Blue"'.[75] Requests for special tunes were met by those competent tearoom musicians. In Ballantynes, 'Granny would usually send me up with a shilling to ask the pianist to "play a tune from the Hebrides". The pianist, a stout lady in pink, always obliged and Granny would clap vigorously as she finished, embarrassing my reserved Mum no end!' recalled Joan Pleasants.[76] Occasionally things could get a little confused. One young woman was remembered for shyly whispering her request for the 'The Wedding of the Painted Doll', from the 1929 film *The Broadway Melody*, whereupon, to her extreme embarrassment, the group burst into the familiar strains of the 'Wedding March' from *Lohengrin*, for a crowded and rather mystified Auckland tearoom.

As well as featuring music in publicity about the store's tearooms, enterprising copy-writers could reflect a modern approach by stressing their scientific approach to nutrition. Nourished by decades of Sir Truby King's rhetoric, and supported by the establishment of domestic science as an integral part of the educational curriculum for girls, an earnest spiel addressed both men and women's increasing interest and anxiety about healthy eating in George Court's campaign to promote and publicise its tearoom:

Your Health Is Made or Unmade at the Dinner Table . . . Patronise a Good Restaurant.

As often has been said, but is worth repeating, our best defence against all diseases is a strong, healthy, well-nourished body. Good, sound, 'High-class' food, and plenty of it is not a luxury: it is an investment in health that will repay itself twenty times a year. Your body is what you make it . . . a composite of the nourishment you give it as food. Supply it with those foods which are natural to it, and it fairly glows with vigorous health . . . health that makes you glad to be alive. Men are, largely, what they eat. The underfed man has an underfed brain. Good food makes good blood. Good blood makes a strong brain, and a strong brain produces good thought. George Court's pride themselves in viewing cooking as an art — and interpreting this art to perfection in their Restaurant and Tearoom — 'Overlooking Auckland'.[77]

Rendell's 'Karo' tearoom, operating on the first floor of the store for about ten years under the management of Mrs J. H. Wood, stated 'only 1st quality materials used in our cooking — Everything is Home Made'.[78]

As well as wholesome ingredients, novelty and variety in food were also given publicity in an effort to attract customers. George Court's advertised oysters in season 'specially selected, professionally opened and perfectly served'.[79] At their tearoom opening it was advertised that 'original dishes often occupy a place on our luncheon

Rendell's and the interior of the Kensington, later the Karo, Tearooms over the store. These were closed by late 1933 and a tearoom opened on the lower ground floor.
C 22587, AUCKLAND WAR MEMORIAL MUSEUM LIBRARY.

menu, and for morning and afternoon tea too. We suggest that tomorrow you try one of the following, just for a change. A club sandwich with a glass of Kentish Ale [a soft drink]; a Devonshire Tea with scones, Homemade Jam and Cream; or perhaps a George Court's Special Sundae.'[80] John Court also offered a special ice-cream sundae, and strawberries and cream, in season, at 9d and 1s. In 1939, they were offering a daily change of lunch menu through the week, including a mixed grill (2s), and 'fillet steak & tomato or peas' (1s 9d).[81]

Six years earlier, Kirkcaldie & Stains' menu had offered raspberries and cream at 9d, but their 'mixed grill' (2s 6d) and 'grilled undercut and chips' (2s) had been significantly dearer, despite Depression conditions. By 1940 a typical bill of fare for George Court's Friday special three-course meal at 1s 6d, offered a prosaic selection of cheaper food, albeit couched in a refined style: 'Tomato or Pea soup with sippets, Fish dishes and delicious salads (fruit and vegetable), Entrées: Haricot mutton, Fricasse of Tripe and onions, Macaroni cheese and our well-known Steak and Kidney Pie; Sweets: Prunes and Rice, Pineapple Flummery, Baked Date Pudding and Sauce; Tea Coffee or Fruit Drink'.[82] The ubiquitous 'Macaroni Cheese' and 'Steak and Kidney Pie' clearly remained popular and economic fare.

Advertising publicity, which promoted the welcoming atmosphere of department stores and their tearooms, needed sensitive monitoring in the inter-war period. John Court's store emblem, appearing in its advertisements, and printed on all its letterheads and accounts, was the swastika, an ancient symbol of prosperity and good fortune.[83] Commenting on the disturbing international scene in Europe, a striking political cartoon, reproduced from *Punch,* appeared in the *New Zealand Herald* on 20 April 1933. Hitler, with General von Hindenburg beside him, proudly held a swastika-topped rod, while behind him the Reichstag burned. Over a few weeks, the use of the swastika by the store diminished rapidly, disappearing from John Court's advertisements completely by the end of May 1933.[84] One of John Court's daughters remembered that 'it was removed from all items at great expense in respect for the feelings of the local Jewish community'.[85] Since it appeared on tearoom china, as well as on carpets in the store, this was a significant concession by the company.

Department stores had to maximise the patronage of their tearooms. Their operating costs were always closely scrutinised, with prices carefully calculated and calibrated against those of other stores. Profitability was not among the leading reasons for maintaining food services, but it was certainly an important factor. In the six months leading up to February 1937, Kirkcaldie & Stains' tearoom recorded the second largest sales in any department of the store; returning £7,598, it was a healthy runner-up to the earnings in furnishings and floor coverings.[86] Surprisingly, the years of World War II were profitable ones for some department store tearooms. The period from 1943 until 1948 was the only time in its 22 years of operation in which George Court's tearoom was ever recorded as making even a marginal profit.[87] Similarly, in 1943 the Farmers' Board of Directors recorded that they 'considered the tearoom profit earned was highly satisfactory, and felt that it reflected great credit on the manner in which the tearoom has been managed by Mrs McKinstry'.[88]

The previous year, when supplies of some foods were rationed and others seasonally scarce, it had been suggested that a farm be purchased to produce fresh vegetables, poultry and eggs for Farmers' tearoom. Apart from the difficulties then being experienced in securing supplies of these important ingredients, and the economic benefit that such an enterprise might bring, this was promoted as an advantageous move for the company from an advertising point of view.[89] No doubt there were memories of John Court's purchase of the idyllic 'Hobson' farm on the banks of Tamaki River, which was stocked with pedigree Friesian cattle and which supplied their tearoom with fresh milk, cream and eggs.[90] Within a month, however, a cautious Farmers' Board had decided against this foray into vertical integration.[91]

Good management through difficult times was a critical factor in determining whether department store tearooms stayed profitable. It is doubtful if any other department store tearoom management was able to rival the record of Miss R. Mahoney, who retired in 1971, after 35 years as manageress of the DIC restaurant in Christchurch:

She did an incredible job during the war. Because of staff shortages she had the vegetables delivered to her home and she and her mother worked through the night to prepare them — often by candlelight because of power cuts. In the morning, the prepared vegetables were delivered to the only cook, Miss Tweedie, and a midday meal was prepared. The DIC fare was so popular that there was often a queue, four deep right back to the fire doors at the end of the restaurant. On Fridays two staff members had to be detailed as queue controllers. The food was good, the prices were right (soup cost 3d, chicken 1/9 and a salad 1/3) and the service was as quick as a limited number of hands and feet could make it.[92]

Maintaining first-class food service when numbers fluctuated throughout each week presented very large tearooms with problems. Still needing to be fully operational on days when shoppers were less likely to come to the city, firms like George Court's tried to build up their Monday clientele by advertising specially priced meals.[93] With entrepreneurial zeal, they encouraged campers to use their facilities in the quiet holiday season after Christmas: 'Situated just a few minutes from the city's motor camp, George Court's great Fourth Floor offers you a restful lounge to await your friends, writing and telephoning facilities, Men's Smoke Room, Ladies' Retiring Room, Men's toilet, Ladies' toilet etc. The cool spacious restaurant is renowned for its perfect cuisine and reasonable charges. Children specially catered for.'[94]

Although most patrons sustaining the tearooms were members of the shopping public, the use of the facility by even a minority of a store's staff contributed to its turnover. Farmers' maintained a separate staff dining room, and later a cafeteria for their employees, where meals were supplied at cost.[95] Beath's, Ballantynes, George Court's, H. & J. Smith's store in Gore, and Milne & Choyce, were among stores that had separate staff cafeterias.[96] In other department stores, public tearooms offered easily accessible and reasonably priced refreshments. Employees in John Court's nearby workrooms in Victoria Building, on the corner of Lorne and Victoria Street East, used the store's tearoom, as did staff members from Smith & Caughey's, who also patronised other city lunch venues as their wages allowed.[97]

Staff were surprisingly long-serving. Flora Wilson began work in H. & J. Smith's tearooms in the 1940s and by the time of her retirement, had worked her way up to be the manager, a position previously held by men.[98] The management of large department store tearooms presented important job opportunities for suitably qualified women. Some were more attractive and sought-after situations than others, especially in relation to working conditions and amenities. In July 1923, the Misses Leonora and Emma Holben were thanked for their management of the Farmers' tearooms.[99] They had been appointed as Tearoom Managers for rival store Milne & Choyce at £450 and £400, respectively, with a £20 dress allowance each.[100] Records indicate that Milne & Choyce's tearooms were 'a decided convenience to our many patrons' and 'a valuable asset to the business in every way'.[101] This affirmation might also have been applied to the capable, tearoom management team of the Misses Holben, still remembered for their skills.[102] They stayed at the Tudor Room through the early years of the Depression, despite a reduction of wages in 1931.[103] Two years later Emma Holben visited Australia to study the new tearooms of Myer's Emporium; in 1935, her elder sister Leonora Holben retired, and was replaced by Miss Armstrong at a salary of £500. Visiting restaurants in Sydney and Melbourne to see the latest trends in management and décor was accepted as an important experience for Milne & Choyce's incoming manageress, but could also result in further expense, as renovations were required to maintain up-to-date facilities.[104] Busy tearoom kitchens could also be extremely dangerous work-places. As the result of one accident in 1927, an assistant in the Tudor Room lost an eye, and received a settlement from Milne & Choyce.[105] Ten years later, £750 was claimed from the same company for another accident in the tearoom kitchen, but the claim was later settled for £130.[106]

Despite the extra outlay required for upgrading equipment, redecorating and sourcing supplies of scarce food items, the glorious heyday of New Zealand department store tearooms extended through the inter-war period and beyond the lean years of World War II. It was not until 1948, after several further changes of staff, that Milne & Choyce's Tudor Room was clearly seen to be in difficulties, losing approx £400 per month. In that year they received an offer to take over their tearoom from Messrs L. & M. Masters, who had recently arrived from England. After several months, however, it was reported that the brothers had changed their minds and were no longer prepared to lease the tearooms.[107] The writing was on the wall. For a few years, managers were engaged on a temporary basis, but the costs of the once proud Tudor Room, capable of catering for more than a quarter of a million patrons a year, could no longer be sustained. In 1951 it was closed after more than 25 years of operation.[108]

The refurbished area became a furniture showroom with 10,000 square feet of floor space devoted to 'all that's best in furniture and furnishing'.[109] The adjacent Reception Hall was converted into a new, successful, but less capacious 'Skyroom' restaurant.[110] In 1952 John Court closed its tearoom, which had increased its seating capacity to over 400, and two years later opened a cafeteria which catered for 200; it used half of the sixth-floor space, the rest being taken by the china department.[111]

Post-war difficulties in department store tearooms did not apply only to Auckland. In 1950, somewhat belatedly, 'a tea lounge and conveniences for ladies as well as a changing room for babies' opened at A. & T. Inglis in Dunedin, but in 1955 that department store shut its doors for good.[112] Kirkcaldie & Stains' tearoom in Wellington was also losing money, despite the boost that events such as the spectacular Italian fashion event had brought. By 1956, private operators had taken over the lease of

When the Tudor Room was closed in 1951, the space was converted into a furniture department. The adjacent reception hall in the annexe became the new Skyroom restaurant. R. S. MILNE.

the tearoom and the coffee lounge. The Steinway grand piano, upon which Frank Crowther had delighted so many with his playing, was revamped in white, to match the décor of the 'Pavilion' restaurant and nightclub.[113] In 1957 Beath's Christchurch store was modernised and redecorated. Their great green and gold restaurant, which the Queen had honoured with her presence only three years before, was replaced by a large fashion salon with 'contemporary décor and clever lighting'.[114]

George Court's too, faced increasing operating losses. At the end of 1953 the tearoom closed on Friday evenings. Approximately £900 of the loss incurred in the tearoom during the previous year was traced to Friday evening opening.[115] By 1956, George Court's had given up the struggle, and the tearoom was resurrected as the new headquarters of the Auckland Travel Club, with a spectacular opening ceremony addressed by Queen Salote of Tonga.[116] In its heyday in the 1960s, the Auckland Travel Club had over 1000 members, with 500 on the waiting list. It might be assumed that at least some of the women club members who made their way to the lifts in George Court's on a Thursday would have provided potential customers for the store. According to one sales assistant, however, many of them would emerge from the elevators and walk straight out of the shop.[117] During the 1960s, Rendell's closed its tearoom on the lower ground floor, when 'space was needed for expansion within the store'.[118] Patterns of shopping in Karangahape Road were clearly changing.

New Zealanders' greatly increased use of cars was resulting in less dependence on public transport.[119] Farmers' new car-parking building on the corner of Wyndham and Hobson Streets had been completed in 1956; in a bold move to capture what was

Farmers' gleaming new coffee machine with staff and customers in the basement coffee bar, opened in the late 1950s. A cup of coffee costs 1s, and capuccino, 1s 3d, with hot chocolate and fruit juices also for sale. 426B, AUCKLAND WAR MEMORIAL MUSEUM LIBRARY.

perceived as the latest American trend for drive-in catering, the 'Top-of-the Park' restaurant was opened there in 1958.[120] Although the main tearoom continued to plod on, other smaller eating spots were also operating in the store. Farmers' set up a new coffee bar in the basement. By the end of 1959 'the profits from the Snack Bar and the new Coffee Bar . . . exceeded the profit shown by our main Dining Room Floor'.[121] The children's playground was roofed over and a coffee bar opened alongside, with a view of the recently opened harbour bridge. This offered more informal eating for parents and children, and new favourites for the youngsters. Vegetables and gravy gave way to cream doughnuts, hot meat pies and sausage rolls with tomato sauce, and potato chips.

By 1960 the 'Top-of-the-Park' restaurant was in financial difficulty. Views of the city, bridge and harbour, even at night, were no longer a sufficient attraction, nor was the

Beath's department store, corner Colombo and Cashel Streets, in 1960. GREEN AND HAHN PHOTOGRAPH. 1988.314.4, CANTERBURY MUSEUM.

opportunity to sit and eat a meal in the car. If one wished to drive to a restaurant there were now establishments in Titirangi or Maungakiekie, which offered comfortable, sophisticated dining, with music and a dance floor as well as panoramic views.[122]

In 1957 the need for change in department store food services had been clearly demonstrated at Milne & Choyce when a coffee bar was opened on the mezzanine floor. A few years later one was situated in the basement, adjacent to the food hall, while in 1961 a 'Men's Coffee Den' was instituted.[123] By 1960, Beath's lower ground floor housed a new coffee bar that could seat 125 and was patronised by more than 2500 people each week. For many patrons, its shipboard décor evoked the shared experience of overseas travel.[124] The convenience of smaller informal eating places close to the main retailing area, yet not actually occupying valuable ground floor space, was now a

A roof was placed over the Farmers' playground area in the late 1950s, creating an all-weather attraction for children. Seating for the adjacent coffee bar can be seen on the far right. G. GRIFFIN.

more realistic option than maintaining a large half-deserted tearoom on the top floor.

Although the new 'Cedar Room' on Smith & Caughey's second floor was opened in late 1958 in association with Otto Groen, the owner of one of Auckland's best restaurants, other department-store tearooms were closing.[125] The Cedar Room was a bold but successful venture, with more than 106,000 customers served in its first year, but it was the exception.[126] With falling patronage, the high costs of providing food services in aging department store buildings ultimately outweighed their advantages to management.

For many years the tearooms had been the high-point of the stores, offering stylish, non-gendered spaces where men, women and children could share together in enjoyable and long-remembered occasions. The waxing and waning of those tearooms paralleled the symbolic rise and fall of the stores themselves.

CONCLUSION

Going Up, Going Down has focused on New Zealand department stores as they reached their mid-twentieth-century heyday. By the early 1980s, despite a generally prosperous retail environment, many of these once great New Zealand institutions were in retreat. By the end of the decade, New Zealand was witnessing the final days of the department store as a symbol of modern life. The earlier image of modernity, so vital for the stores' success, was fast fading and the stores' commercial fortunes were in decline. Only a few of the great enterprises of former years, including Ballantynes, Kirkcaldie & Stains, Smith & Caughey's, Arthur Barnett, and H. & J. Smith, surfaced from these tough times. Increasingly, department stores were seen as bastions of formal, slightly stuffy tradition, not of newness and innovation.

Farmers', for example, for many years the self-proclaimed largest department store in the Dominion, celebrated its seventy-fifth anniversary in 1984 with a massive marketing campaign. Yet behind all the advertising publicity and hype lay a struggle to hold on to consumers' dollars and the old firm's place in people's imaginations. This great retailing enterprise was run from what a magazine reporter described as a 'modest (some would say dated) wood-panelled office on the first floor of Farmer's flag-ship, the famous Hobson St building in Auckland'. Far from being a beacon of modernity, the store was said to stand out 'like a pastor in a massage parlour'.[1] Only a few years later the mighty Hobson St site was sold off, as the company transformed its brand. Once strongly identified with its one-of-a-kind central store, Farmers' became increasingly associated with a proliferation of local branches, many of them anchor tenants in the department stores' *bête noire*, the suburban shopping mall.

Of course the stores had always faced financial challenges. Even in the 1920s, the growth of department stores worldwide had not been stress free, unchallenged or inevitable. Competition from cut-price chain stores, together with the heavy overheads involved in advertising, maintaining large buildings, high staffing levels, and a variety of services, had dogged department stores throughout their operation.[2] According to one Australian business analyst, 'most department stores never fully recovered from the crisis of the 1930s Depression . . . . By the late 1950s, many . . . were in rapid decline.'[3] It was clear that the effect of more than two decades of local threats and challenges was beginning to weigh heavily upon the retailing success of New Zealand's department stores. Exchange and import restrictions imposed in the late 1930s had dried up the plentiful flow of goods with which local department stores could stock their shelves.[4] Shortages persisted during World War II, price stabilisation was established to avert inflation, and, in 1942, rationing of goods was introduced.[5]

After the war, import restrictions continued. This interventionist policy was a significant problem for a small country with limited population and resources, situated at great distance from international markets. New Zealand struggled to develop and sustain domestic manufacturing industries. Relatively small companies, such as fashion garment manufacturers, could not afford to take risks and generally operated within clearly defined limits in order to be profitable. This resulted in a universal criticism of the 'sameness' of goods on display in department stores, which, of necessity, stocked items mostly of New Zealand manufacture.[6] The stores, many undercapitalised, found it hard to survive, let alone to make a profit while such a restrictive climate prevailed. As the chairman of George Court's Board of Directors stated: 'Business . . . could be much better if it were permitted to be. A strait jacket is not conducive to comfort nor an encouragement to activity.'[7]

Department store managers faced high costs maintaining massive, inner-city buildings. Escalating overheads meant there was an urgent need to attract customers into the central city, yet the constraints of the store buildings themselves often made expansion difficult or impossible. When John Court incorporated the roof garden into its tearoom, ensuring greater seating capacity, the kitchen could not be extended to cope with the extra workload.[8] There was literally no room to increase the space. A public façade of safety and modernity might have been maintained for customers, but staff often knew differently. Heavily used equipment could become out of date, and poor working conditions in aging buildings resulted in a high turnover of personnel. The ever-rising wage bill was another cost to be met by department store management.

The story of the stores' decline, however, isn't simply a study in economic history. Demographic shifts and cultural changes are also significant. By the 1960s the post-war

LynnMall still holds pride of place as Auckland's oldest shopping mall —
its earliest example of the new 'cathedrals of consumption'. E. LAURENSON.

population boom was beginning to make its presence felt in new retail environments.
Housing developments mushroomed, and a slow but steady movement of commerce
away from the central business districts began. Auckland, for instance, experienced
major difficulties in providing effective public transport within a city which extended far
beyond its original narrow isthmus. Inner-city department stores became increasingly
remote from the informal patterns of suburban life. People no longer felt it necessary
to dress up for a day in town, or even go to town at all. Conveniently located American-
style shopping malls offered more appealing options for their customers. Shopping
in an array of specialty shops with a variety of merchandise and services, within a
comfortable and more casual setting complete with plenty of free parking spaces was
the latest trend; it was far more convenient than a trip to an inner-city department
store. Some stores, most notably Farmers', opened branches in malls, recognising the
role such centres were to perform in reaching burgeoning suburban populations. The
ultimate freeing-up of trading restrictions during the 1980s came too late for many

department stores. Smaller fashion boutiques, some opened by erstwhile department-store buyers, could operate more flexibly with lower overheads, less risk, and more attention to individual customers. Together with specialty chain stores selling women's clothing in suburban malls, they provided competition in the fashion stakes that was difficult to match. Houseware stores, presenting stylish accessories to match new and ever-changing lifestyles of affluence, appeared on the scene to challenge the department stores' role as provider of household linen.

Another constant image presented by the stores had been that of the middle-class gentleman. It had served them well through the years of New Zealand's conformist male fashion. When this conservative style changed, department stores struggled to replace it with a variety of images. The diversity of men's fashion was unable, either physically or economically, to be contained within the menswear department. The informal blazers or sports jackets and trousers, were, in their own way, imposing a new uniformity on men's casual fashion, and were replacing suits for many occasions. By the end of the 1950s, other images of masculinity were emerging. 'Ever since the teenager first became visible in the sales-talk of marketers and advertisers in the 1950s, young men . . . have rarely been out of sight of the consumer economy.'[9] The growth of male boutiques and specialty stores reflected new and sophisticated design and marketing technologies, together with the changing lifestyles of a generation of young men who looked beyond the confines of department store menswear sections for their fashion needs.

Redmer Yska has described the 1950s as years of change for New Zealand, when a new social category — teenagers — became the 'most visible symbol of the new consumer dream'.[10] Department stores struggled to find a key to the world of teenage fashion. Some tackled the problem head on. Milne & Choyce's 'Tweens' Section' produced some increased sales.[11] Kirkcaldie & Stains opened a teenage department in 1953, drawing some of its stock from other departments.[12] James Smith's however, was still promoting their children's department as the place to find 'cute sub-teen and Teenager party frocks' at sale prices in 1959.[13] In that same year, Farmers' offered look-alike 'jeans for mother and daughter'.[14] Whether jeans just like mother wore were what up-and-coming teenagers would wish for, in an age when Elvis was 'king of rock'n'roll', was debatable. Teenagers were not generally shopping for clothes with mother, but were earning and spending their own money.

Department stores' efforts to remake their image for 1950s teenagers suffered from their association with the provision of children's clothing and school uniforms in the lean times of the 1940s. It was difficult to discard the images of restriction, rationing and 'no frills'. The stores' efforts to retain their adult customers had allowed little scope for attending creatively to the interests of those who were to be their future consumers. Children's future patronage as customers was integral to the stores' survival and the focus on children during the 1920s and 1930s had been important in securing adults customers in later decades. By the 1940s the 'golden weather' had ended, and a scarcity of toys, clothing and organised amusement began; with dwindling stocks, staff shortages and electricity cuts, there was little energy or material for annual bursts of creativity on the scale of former years. The spell had been broken. Experiences which in tough times had once seemed new and modern — even breathtaking — had become commonplace for 1950s children. The stores were losing their ability to introduce children to a world of fantasy and excitement, and no longer represented such a conjunction with modernity. Whole new genres of children's literature, movies, and a flood of toys were to enrich children's lives, even before the advent of television in the 1960s.

With one or two exceptions, there seemed little attention given to planning for children's continued loyalty in many New Zealand department stores.[15] Hay's and Farmers' were aware of children as consumers, not necessarily of goods, but of new experiences. The latter's basic policy as stated in 1953 had been 'catch them young and bring them often, for they are the customers of the future'.[16] Despite their best efforts, and the affection with which many remember Hay's roof-top 'Joyland' in Christchurch, or Farmers' store in Hobson Street, with its pet shop, playground and tearoom, this policy ultimately relied on the stores' continuing ability to supply new visions of modernity.[17]

Department store tearooms lost their place as the acme of style. Post-war eating places proliferated and post-war migrants from Europe began to influence local eating habits.[18] Whether one wished to eat in 'a world of Parisian basements, or to the back street rendezvous of the underworld characters one sees in a Humphrey Bogart movie', or be surrounded by a 'costly décor . . . comparable in many cases to a high class New York or London restaurant', such places were now within reach.[19] Why go to the top floor of a department store only to be seated in a vast half-empty dining room, when there were so many other new and exciting venues? Already, in the prosperous 1950s, overseas travel was becoming an option for more New Zealanders. A journalist writing an early restaurant guide was confident enough to address his readers with 'quite a few of you may have been lucky enough to actually visit Europe and see for yourself the true continental night rendezvous'.[20] Cost was no longer as significant to diners in the relatively affluent 1950s when 'Fillet Mignon' and 'Chicken-in-a-Basket' appeared on the menu rather than the economies of 'Haricot Mutton' and 'Fricassee of Tripe and Onions'.

Towards the end of 1957, a brief article in the *New Zealand Herald* indicated the changing patterns of fashion. 'Fashions normally means clothes, but not always. The latest to reach Auckland is in the coffee houses. Proprietors, casting round for something to enhance the coffee itself have found it — in art.' The names Milan Mrkusich, Dennis Turner, Michael Nicholson and Freda Simmonds were listed as those whose work had been exhibited in local coffee bars. 'Another, from whose walls oils, prints and tapestries hang, provides a small library for patrons. "If ze meal is dull," he says, "zey can at least be reading."' The reporter continued: 'perhaps not surprisingly — where at first the new coffee-house proprietors were predominantly immigrants, their art-conscious successors are mainly New Zealanders'.[21] The art on display in those 1950 coffee bars represented a very different world from that of Sydney Lough Thompson's depictions of New Zealand mountain scenery, exhibited for sale in Beath's tearoom in 1925, or the gilt-framed Van der Velden oil paintings once selected by William Ballantyne to grace his firm's lounge and tearoom.[22] In the department stores, the security of the traditional had taken the place of the excitement of the modern.

With a final nostalgic glance at the paintings on those panelled walls, and a fleeting look back at the fronded palms and deserted piano, those ranks of tables and their empty cake stands, it is time to leave the grand tearooms and go down in the lift for the last time. The double doors shut with a clash of finality. There is a sober quietness, even a sadness, as the lift attendant intones the passing floors, but the lift does not stop as those glimpses of former glorious fashion, of magical experiences, of a profusion of luxurious goods, move quickly past us. Before we know it, we are back on the ground floor and moving out through the main doors with a steady flow of other customers.

The magic promises of this world of colour and light, which department stores had capitalised into successful business ventures, no longer were persuasive. Consumers' aspirations remained strong, but their desires were being satisfied in reference to different aesthetic and commercial values. The department store lady, hatted and gloved, with her charge card and dainty tearoom lunch has given way to the mall-shopper, snacking on food-court sushi, and laden with carry-bags from a variety of chain stores in the latest 'cathedral of consumption'.

NOTES

.⤝

INTRODUCTION

1   'Gary Hoover's Top Five Ideas', CNNMoney, online, 12 February 2002, http://money.cnn.com

2   Elizabeth Light, 'Department Stores', *Retail*, September 2000, p.24. 'Grandes Dames' identified as Smith & Caughey's, Kirkcaldie & Stains, Ballantynes and Arthur Barnett.

3   Geoffrey Crossick and Serge Jaumain, eds, *Cathedrals of Consumption: the European Department Store, 1850–1939*, Brookfield, V'I', 1999.

4   *Otago Daily Times* (ODT), 18 August 1866, p.3.

5   *Wellington Independent*, 28 November 1863, p.2; *Evening Post* (EP), 27 February 1929, p.9.

6   R. C. J. Stone, 'Auckland Business and Businessmen in the 1880s', PhD thesis, University of Auckland, 1969, p.223.

7   Angela Caughey, *An Auckland Network*, Auckland, 1988, p.118.

8   There was no partner named 'Leeds'; this was a pun. Malcolm Kay, *Inside Story of Farmers': First Complete Record of the Marvellous Growth of Laidlaw Leeds and the Farmers' Trading Co. Ltd*, Auckland, 1953, p.22.

9   EP, 29 November 1920, p.11.

10 Smith & Caughey's and Milne & Choyce each purchased blocks of adjacent land in the late 1920s; in 1923, George Court's acquired a site on the corner of France and Cross Streets directly behind their store in Karangahape Road. Three years later, their new corner building was opened, *Auckland Star* (AS), 23 November 1926, p.9.

11 Anna Rogers, *Earthquakes*, Wellington, 1996, p.5.

12 *Daily Telegraph* (DT), 2 March 1931, p.6; DT, 27 March 1931, pp.3, 4.

13 AS, 14 October 1926, p.14.

14 Alison Adburgham, *Shops and Shopping 1800–1914: Where, and in What Manner the Well-dressed Englishwoman Bought her Clothes*, London, 1964, pp.137–41; Michael B. Miller, *The Bon Marché: Bourgeois Culture and the Department Store, 1869–1920*, Princeton, 1981, pp.25–6; Gareth Shaw, 'The Evolution and Impact of Large-scale Retailing in Britain', in John Benson and Gareth Shaw, eds, *The Evolution of Retail Systems c.1800–1914*, Leicester, 1992, p.138.

15 Jodine Lyons, 'The Grand Magasins of the South: the World of Dunedin Department Stores 1890–1960', BA(Hons) Research Essay, University of Otago, 1999, p.1.

16 M. E. Thomson, *Beath's Centennial: 1860–1960*, Christchurch, 1960, p.[17].

17 Peter Ackroyd, *London: the Biography*, London, 2000, p.402; Victoria De Grazia, 'Introduction', in Victoria De Grazia and Ellen Furlough, eds, *The Sex of Things: Gender and Consumption in Historical Perspective*, Berkeley, 1996, p.4.

18 John Benson, *The Rise of Consumer Society in Britain, 1880–1980*, London, 1994, p.27.

19 Peter N. Stearns, *Consumerism in World History: The Global Transformation of Desire*, London, 2001, p.138.

20 Informal conversation with Yvonne Sanders, 2 April 2002.

21 John Fiske, 'Commodities and Culture', in *Understanding Popular Culture*, Boston, 1989, pp.23–48; Gail Reekie, *Temptations: Sex, Selling and the Department Store*, St Leonards, 1993, pp.179–80.

22 Elizabeth Kowaleski-Wallace, *Consuming Subjects: Women, Shopping and Business in the Eighteenth Century*, New York, 1997; Claire Walsh, 'The Newness of the Department Store: a View from the Eighteenth Century', in Crossick and Jaumain, p.45; Neil McKendrick, John Brewer and J. H. Plumb, eds, *The Birth of a Consumer Society: the Commercialization of Eighteenth-Century England*, Bloomington, 1982.

23 Thorstein Veblen, *The Theory of the Leisure Class: An Economic Study of Institutions* (1899), new edn, London, 1970.

24 T. J. Jackson Lears and Richard Wightman Fox, 'Introduction' in Richard Wightman Fox and T. J. Jackson Lears, eds, *The Culture of Consumption: Critical Essays in American History 1880–1980,* New

York, 1983, pp.x–xi.

25 T. J. Jackson Lears, 'From Salvation to Self-Realization: Advertising and the Therapeutic Roots of the Consumer Culture, 1880–1930' in Wightman Fox and Jackson Lears, p.3.

26 Becky Conekin, Frank Mort and Chris Waters, 'Introduction', in Becky Conekin, Frank Mort and Chris Waters, eds, *Moments of Modernity: Reconstructing Britain 1945–1964,* London, 1999, p.9.

27 J. H. Plumb, 'The Acceptance of Modernity', in McKendrick, Brewer and Plumb, p.334.

28 Minutes of Board of Directors, 9 August 1961, MS 1400, Box 2, Item (4), Farmers' Trading Company Archives (FTCA), Auckland Institute and Museum Library (AR) (hereafter Minutes of Board of Directors); Minutes of Board, 27 July 1961, MS 0251, Box 3, Item (2), Milne & Choyce Records (M&CR), Fletcher Challenge Archives, Penrose (FCA) (hereafter Minutes of Board); Minutes of Board, 22 February 1962.

29 Crossick and Jaumain; Stuart Ewen and Elizabeth Ewen, *Channels of Desire: Mass Images and the Shaping of American Consciousness*, New York, 1982, pp.69, 193–5; William R. Leach, *Land of Desire: Merchants, Power, and the Rise of the New American Culture,* New York, 1993, pp.39–41.

ONE: GROUND FLOOR — GOING UP

1 'Gully Boy', *Metro,* January 1989, p.60.

2 AS, 8 December 1921, p.10; Jim Sullivan, *One Hundred Years of Loyalty: The Story of Arthur Barnett Ltd 1903–2003,* Dunedin, 2003, p.37.

3 A. H. McLintock, ed., *An Encyclopaedia of New Zealand*, Vol.3, Wellington, 1966, p.444.

4 EP, 17 November 1904, p.9.

5 Ian Hunter, *Robert Laidlaw: Man for Our Time: Triumph Against All Odds*, Auckland, 1999.

6 In 1936, trams replaced buses on the route from Karangahape Road, according to Kay, pp.171–3; trolley buses later replaced the trams. Trolley buses were operating from Queen to Hobson Streets by 1939.

7 *New Zealand Herald* (NZH), 15 April 1932, p.19.

8 'Where Shall I park in Town?', [Leaflet, nd], MS 1400, Box 15, Folder 105, FTCA, AR. In a later pamphlet, space is offered for 160 cars as well as a motorists' service station, an extension dated 1930 in Hunter, p.195.

9 Katie Pickles, 'Workers and Workplaces — Industry and Modernity', in John Cookson and Graeme Dunstall, *Southern Capital: Christchurch: Towards a City Biography 1850–2000*, Christchurch, 2000, p.158.

10 Ibid.

11 'Auckland Scrapbook, November 1959–April 1960', p.30, Auckland Research Centre, Auckland City Library (AC).

12 Gerald Whiting, *Department Store*, London, 1979, p.6.

13 NZH, 16 April 1932, p.9.

14 Louise Shaw, 'Hallenstein Brothers and Company 1876–1906, the Early Years of Mass Retailing in New Zealand', PGDipAAs (History) research essay, Otago University, 1994, p.34.

15 Gordon Parry, *Retailing Century: The First 100 Years of the D.I.C. Ltd*, Dunedin, 1984, p.32.

16 Gordon D. Robertson, 'Adventure in Merchandising: A Financial and Merchandising History of the Farmers' Trading Company Limited for the Period 1909–1939', MCom thesis, University of Auckland, 1967, p.96.

17 L. Frank Baum, *The Art of Decorating Dry Goods Windows and Interiors*, Chicago, 1900, and *The Show Window*, a periodical first issued in 1897, cited in Leach, *Land of Desire*, pp.59–60.

18 Minutes of Board, August 1925.

19 AS, 14 October 1926, p.14.

20 Russell English, 'JCL Building and Services', unpublished notes, 2002, p.1.

21 Sullivan, p.37.

22 Lyons, p.45.

23 Gordon Ogilvie, *Ballantynes: The Story of Dunstable House, 1854–2004*, Christchurch, 2004, p.76.

24 NZH, 6 March 1948, p.12.

25 Minutes of Board, October 1947, p.540; *The Story of a Store*, Pacific Film Unit, c.1949, Christchurch, New Zealand Film Archives, Wellington.

26 'Decorations were a Headache: a Window-Dresser's Views on Xmas', *New Zealand Listener* (NZL), 14, 340, 28 December 1946, p.11.

27 William R. Leach, 'Transformation in a Culture of Consumption: Women and Department Stores, 1890-1925', *Journal of American History*, 71, 1984, p.325.

28 Leach, *Land of Desire*, p.63.

29   Minutes of Board, 14 April 1932, p.174; Shona Caughey, *Smith & Caughey Limited: The Times of Our Life 1880–1980*, Auckland, 1980, p.24; David McGill, *Wellington: Capital Century*, Wellington, 2003, pp.111, 113; English, p.2; NZH, 15 April 1932, p.12;

30   NZH, 15 April 1932, p.11.

31   NZH, 16 April 1932, p.10.

32   'George Court Having the Last Laugh', p.6; NZH, 18 April 1932, p.10.

33   Pickles, p.158.

34   Belle Robertson Avery, 'Meet me at Lunchtime: 1940s', *New Zealand Memories*, 26, October/November 2000, pp.14–17.

35   Informal conversation with Mrs Gordon Sinclair, 5 July 2002.

36   F. Rogers to H. Laurenson, 22 November 2002.

37   Bryan Burton, interviewed by author, 24 October 2002. Also Bryan Burton, 'Some Recollections of the Farmers' Trading Co Ltd', unpublished notes, Auckland, 2002.

38   *40 Years of Progress Winter Catalogue,* June 1949, MS 1400, Box 16, FTCA, AR. The cover has a woman in sensible coat, hat, gloves and handbag. Inside the back cover, heavy brown jute cow and horse covers are advertised.

39   Pauline J. Wood, *Kaiapoi: A Search for Identity*, Rangiora, 1993, pp.105–6.

40   In 1882–1888, Te Mete Raua Ko Kauwhe advertised regularly in the monthly Maori language *Te Korimako*, that 'goods over 20/- would be sewn in canvas and delivered freight-free to any part of the country approachable directly from Auckland', S. Caughey, p.5.

41   Julia Millen, *Kirkcaldie & Stains: A Wellington Story*, Wellington, 2000, p.55.

42   10 June 1929, 'Press Cuttings 1925–29', MS 1400, Box 22, Folder 1, FTCA, AR; Minutes of Board of Directors, October 1920.

43   *Farmers' Trading Co., Ltd. Auckland: Catalogue No.9*, Auckland, 1927, p.2. This typical catalogue has 550 pages.

44   'Form Letters', [nd], MS 1400, Box 15, Folder 105, FTCA, AR.

45   DT, 14 March 1931, p.10; DT, 21 March 1931, p.4.

46   NZH Supplement, 25 May 1935, p.11.

47   Parry, p.32.

48   Keith F. Douglas, *H & J Smith: Traders for 100 Years*, Invercargill, 2000, p.12.

49   Jean Howe, interviewed by author, 7 August 2002.

50   Millen, p.209; Ogilvie, p.210.

51   Ibid., pp.80–82, 208–9.

52   Ogilvie, pp.60–61.

53   Sullivan, pp.46–7, 55.

54   Susan Porter Benson, 'Palaces of Consumption and Machine for Selling: The American Department Store, 1880–1940', *Radical History Review*, 21, Fall 1979, pp.208–9; Susan Porter Benson, *Counter Cultures: Saleswomen, Managers, and Customers in American Department Stores, 1890–1940,* Urbana, Illinois, 1986, p.44.

55   Janet Frame, *An Autobiography*, Auckland, 1989, p.231.

56   Ogilvie, p.228.

57   Boys would have worn caps, instead of the ubiquitous hats. J. S. Milne issued an order that all men employed by the company had to wear a hat, R. S. Milne, interviewed by author, 14 August 2002. Ballantyne's male staff were expected to wear hats to and from work, Ogilvie, p.103.

58   *Rules and Regulations: Smith & Caughey, Ltd. Auckland, N.Z.,* Auckland, 1931, p.4; 'If you asked female staff to wear other than black you had to pay for it — cleaning etc,' Milne, 2002.

59   Ogilvie, pp.103, 104.

60   *Rules: John Court, Ltd. Auckland,* Auckland, [1920], p.17.

61   Women shop assistant's uniforms were later changed to brown, then wine and, later again, blue. Millen, p.140.

62   AS, 24 January 1929, p.10.

63   Paul H. Nystrom, *Retail Selling and Store Management*, New York, 1925, p.61, cited in Rachel Bowlby, *Carried Away: the Invention of Modern Shopping*, London, 2000, p.57.

64   Ewen and Ewen; Leach, *Land of Desire*; Gail Reekie, *Temptations: Sex, Selling and the Department Store*; Mary Louise Roberts, 'Gender, Consumption, and Commodity Culture', *American Historical Review*, 103, 1, 1998, p.819.

65   Jill Greenfield, Sean O'Connell and Chris Reid, 'Gender, Consumer Culture and the Middle Class Male, 1918–39', in Alan Kidd and David Nicholls, eds *Gender, Civic Culture and Consumerism: Middle-Class Identity in Britain, 1800–1940*, Manchester, 1999, pp.183–97.

66   Steve Garlick, 'Men, Clothing and Identity:

Fashioning Masculine Subjectivities', *Sites*, 37, 1999, pp.64–82; Sue Tait, 'Advertising, Cultural Criticism and Mythologies of the Male Body', in Robin Law, Hugh Campbell and John Dolan, eds, *Masculinities in Aotearoa/New Zealand*, Palmerston North, 1999, pp.189–213; Frazer Andrewes, 'The Man in the Grey Flannel Suit: White-collar Masculinity in Post-war New Zealand', in Caroline Daley and Deborah Montgomerie, eds, *The Gendered Kiwi*, Auckland, 1999, pp.191–212; Frazer Andrewes, 'Representations of Masculinity in Postwar New Zealand, 1945–1960', MA thesis, University of Auckland, 1995.

67 Porter Benson, *Counter Cultures*, p.75; Benson's chapter on 'Managing Department-Store Customers' is subtitled 'An Adamless Eden'.

68 Danielle Sprecher, 'The Right Appearance: Representations of Fashion, Gender, and Modernity in New Zealand, 1918–1939', MA thesis, The University of Auckland, 1997, pp.36–7.

69 Leach, 'Transformation in a Culture of Consumption', p.331.

70 Ogilvie, p.27.

71 June 1874 was the date when Charlotte and Mary Jane Milne moved from their smaller shop in Wyndham Street to the larger drapery business in Cheapside House, on the corner of Queen Street and Wellesley Street East; NZH Supplement, 26 September 1900, p.3.

72 *The Cyclopedia of New Zealand: Vol. 3, Canterbury Provincial District*, Christchurch, 1903, p.301.

73 *Spring & Summer Catalogue 1888–9* [cover], S. Caughey, p.7; NZH, 27 December 1894, p.4.

74 William Caughey, interviewed by author, 30 July 2002; AS, 16 December 1916, p.23.

75 'New premises for Messrs John Court Ltd., are very near completion at the corner of Queen or [sic] Victoria streets . . . The roof is flat and is to be used as a tea garden'. *N. Z. Building Progress*, October 1916, pp.757–8; AS, 6 December 1916, p.4.

76 'Luncheon Menu: John Court Ltd' [back cover], [1939].

77 *Auckland Chamber of Commerce Journal*, 15 September 1933, p.5; NZH, 1 September 1933, p.13.

78 AS, 30 December 1939, p.10.

79 AS, 28 December 1939, p.11.

80 NZH, 6 January 1937, p.15.

81 Milne, 2002.

82 Millen, p.144.

83 *Rydges Retail Merchandising Course*, Sydney, 1937, p.16, cited in Gail Reekie, 'Impulsive Women, Predictable Men: Psychological Constructions of Sexual Difference in Sales Literature to 1930', *Australian Historical Studies*, 97, October 1991, p.367.

84 EP, 11 December 1929, p.21.

85 *Draper*, April 1904, p.125; May 1915, p.129; October 1921, p.447, cited in Gail Reekie, 'Impulsive Women, Predictable Men', pp.366–7.

86 *Press*, 5 August 1925, p.7.

87 NZH, 13 September 1932, p.12.

88 EP, 2 October 1929, p.5.

89 NZH Supplement, 9 December 1939, p.7.

90 ODT, 7 February 1925, p.3.

91 NZH, 23 July 1934, p.12.

92 DT, 22 November 1920, p.7.

93 *Press*, 6 May 1925, p.3.

94 AS, 11 May 1935, p.9. This intertextuality continues in George Court's advertising for their tearooms, 'A room with a view', echoing the title of E. M. Forster's 1908 novel, NZH Supplement, 25 May 1935, p.17; the intertextuality of religious and cultural belief was used in other advertisements such as 'the wisest men are ordering suits for Xmas now from John Court Ltd'.

95 Garlick, p.66.

96 AS, 20 February 1940, p.13.

97 Frank Mort, *Cultures of Consumption: Masculinities and Social Space in Late Twentieth-Century Britain*, London, 1996, p.138.

98 *Auckland Chamber of Commerce Journal*, 15 September 1933, p.2.

99 Ibid., p.5; JCL's 'newly completed men's shop — until recently the department for Boys' and Children's wearables, open today', NZH, 1 September 1933, p.13.

100 *Auckland Chamber of Commerce Journal*, 15 September 1933, p.22.

101 Hugh Wright, 'New Zealanders Well Dressed', *Auckland Chamber of Commerce Journal*, 15 September 1933, p.6.

102 *Press*, 29 September 1932, p.9.

103 *Press*, 7 September 1932, p.5.

104 Garlick, p.74.

105 ODT, 4 September 1925, p.3.

106 Millen, pp.137–38.

107 NZH, 20 April 1932, p.12.

108 DT, 22 November 1920, p.7.

109 'Buy in November and ease the strain in December', 1923, pp.[8–9], MS 1400, Box 15, FTCA, AR.

110 *Farmers' Catalogue No.9*, p.431.

111 Suit prices dropped in the early 1930s, depending on the quality of fabric. John Court Ltd was advertising 'Fine quality navy serge suits to measure — £5', NZH, 9 April 1932, p.8. George Court's price remained at £3 17s 6d for most of the 1930s.

112 *Press*, 2 December 1929, p.9.

113 Minutes of Board, February 1934.

114 AS, 11 May 1935, p.9.

115 NZH, 2 July 1935, p.13.

116 NZH,13 August 1935, p.15.

117 EP, 10 December 1925, p.13.

118 J. T. McCorkindale, 'Auckland Men and Their Clothes', *Auckland Chamber of Commerce Journal*, 15 September 1933, p.4; advertisement for 'Milne & Choyce The Store for Men', p.3.

119 Millen, p.141

120 Minutes of Board, February 1944, p.443; March 1944, p.445.

121 *Press*, 13 December 1929, p.6. In 1929, newly established James Hay's was a subsidiary of Macky Logan Caldwell's, a manufacturing and wholesale warehouse. 'Maclone' was their brand-name.

122 EP, 11 December 1929, p.21.

123 NZH, 20 July 1934, p.16.

124 Ogilvie, p.97.

125 Millen, p.147; Parry, p.45.

126 AS, 10 October 1945, p.8; 27 October 1945, p.8.

127 NZH, 11 September 1944, p.7.

128 Ogilvie, p.83.

129 AS, 12 September 1944, p.7.

130 AS, 17 April 1951, p.8.

131 'Advertising Scrapbook, 25 October 1950–10 June 1952', AS 8 o'clock edition, 5 January 1952, NZMS 515, George Court Archives (GCA), Special Collections Department, AC.

132 J. R. Rendell, 'Are Men Becoming More Clothes-Conscious?', *Auckland Chamber of Commerce Journal*, 15 September 1933, p.2: Merchandising Manager's Report, 19 September 1953, NZMS 515, Box 6, GCA, Special Collections Department, AC.

133 NZH, 28 November 1951, p.4.

134 G. E. Wood, *The Wordsmiths: a Study of Advertising Practices in New Zealand with Particular Relevance to Newspaper Advertising*, Wellington, 1964, p.42.

135 EP, 20 December 1959, p.20.

136 B. H. Easton, *Consumption in New Zealand 1954–5 to 1964–5*, Wellington, 1967, p.27.

137 Easton, p.12.

138 EP, 12 September 1955, p.14.

139 G. T. Bloomfield, *New Zealand: A Handbook of Historical Statistics*, Boston, 1984, p.248.

140 Tim Edwards, *Men in the Mirror: Men's Fashion, Masculinity and Consumer Society*, London, 1997, p.102; Garlick, p.77.

141 Frank Mort, 'The Commercial Domain: Advertising and the Cultural Management of Demand', in Conekin, Mort and Waters, p.61.

142 *Hallenstein Bros. Ltd.: 110th Anniversary*, Dunedin, 1984, p.2.

143 AS, 27 November 1957, p.7.

144 NZH Supplement, 28 November 1958, p.11.

145 AS, 22 October 1935, p.16; AS 22 October 1935, p.19.

146 Minutes of Board of Directors, November 1954.

147 Roger Mirams and Gordon O'Shea, 'Auckland Going Up: the Longest [Farmers'] Escalator', *Pacific Magazine 9*, Pacific Films, Auckland, c.1955, New Zealand Film Archives, Wellington.

148 Rob MacGregor, *Around N.Z. in Eighty Cups*, 2nd edn [196–], p.3.

149 Brian O'Connor, interviewed by author, 17 October 2002.

TWO: FIRST FLOOR — MANTLE SHOWROOM, MILLINERY, MANCHESTER AND MERCERY

1 Frame, p.232.

2 Milne, 2002.

3 Jean Howe, interviewed by author, 7 August 2002. Jean continued to work in Smith & Caughey's first floor mantle showroom until after her marriage in 1943. A mantle is a sleeveless cloak or covering.

4 NZH, 1 October 1910, p.4.

5 DT, 30 November 1920, p.7.

6 *Press*, 30 April 1925, p.11.

7 ODT, 4 September 1925, p.2.

8 Reekie, *Temptations: Sex, Selling and the Department Store*.

9 Porter Benson, *Counter Cultures*, p.108.

10 *Dry Goods Economist*, 15 August 1908, p.3, cited in Leach, 'Transformation in a Culture of Consumption', p.327.

11 Jerome Koerber, quoted in *Merchants' Record and Show Window*, February 1912, cited in Leach, *Land of*

Desire, p.91. Emphasis in original.

12   In 1886, Andrew Caughey went to London and appointed Messrs Beath Schiess and Co. as the firm's fashion buyers. The following year William Smith also went to London and bought £11,000 worth of merchandise. Buying direct caused some ill-feeling among Auckland wholesalers. S. Caughey, p.7.

13   Garibaldis were variants on the loose shirts worn by Garibaldi and his followers; the DIC advertised 'Nobby Choker Necklets', EP, 12 December 1925, p.14; Milne & Choyce's slogan, Milne, 2002.

14   NZH, 5 September 1935, p.18.

15   EP, 20 November 1920, p.10.

16   EP, 10 December 1925, p.13.

17   *Press*, 4 August 1925, p.11.

18   ODT, 21 February 1925, p.7.

19   *The City of Enterprise, 1889–1923: A Brief Account of the Amazing Growth of One of the Outposts of Empire and a Tribute to the Initiative of the Founder of One of Its Largest Mercantile Houses*, Auckland, 1923, p.[44].

20   S. Caughey, p.31.

21   NZH, 12 August 1933, p.12.

22   Howe, 2002.

23   Minutes of Board, January 1922, p.20.

24   NZH Supplement, 25 August 1923, p.16.

25   Leaflet, [nd], MS 1400, Box 15, Folder 107, FTCA, AR; NZH, 16 December 1927, p.23.

26   Minutes of Board, March 1925, p.25.

27   Annual Report for year ending 31 July 1925, MS 0254 Box 1, Item (1), M&CR, FCA.

28   NZH, 23 October 1935, p.4.

29   Sullivan, p.53.

30   Minutes of Board, June 1939, p.337.

31   Minutes of Board, March 1943, p.419.

32   AS, 1 July 1935, p.15.

33   NZH, 31 July 1935, p.23; AS, 24 August 1935, p.9.

34   Milne, 2002.

35   Erik Olssen, 'Truby King and the Plunket Society: an Analysis of a Prescriptive Ideology', *New Zealand Journal of History*, 15, 1, 1981, pp.3–23.

36   *Auckland Industrial and Mining Exhibition: Opened December 1st 1898: Official Handbook and Catalogue*, Auckland, 1898, pp.172–4; Sandra Coney, 'Marianne Smith', in *The Dictionary of New Zealand Biography, Volume Four, 1921–1940*, Wellington, 1998, pp.483–4.

37   AS, 14 October 1926, p.14.

38   Kathleen Grattan, 'A Century of Fashion 1866–1966: Milne & Choyce', *Journal of the Auckland Historical Society*, 8, 1966, pp.10–15.

39   *The Cyclopedia of New Zealand: Vol.4, Otago and Southland Provincial Districts*, Christchurch, 1905, p.301.

40   Ogilvie, p.95, states the shop has usually employed the plural form of the name without an apostrophe since 1917.

41   K. A. Tucker, *Milne & Choyce: A One Hundred Year Business History, 1867–1967*, Auckland, 1968, pp.1–3. Tucker's research establishes 1867 rather than 1866 as the opening date of the store.

42   Coney, p.483, notes that Marianne and her husband William sailed to New York in 1874 where William had a job in 'a drapery store'. They returned to Belfast in 1879; S. Caughey, p.1, states that William worked for 'A. T. Stewart and Co.'.

43   W. H. Smith & A. C. Caughey bought land in Newmarket from Alfred Buckland in March 1884 and constructed a Newmarket branch of their business; Dinah Holman, *Newmarket Lost and Found*, Auckland, 2001, p.128; '[t]here was also a branch in Karangahape Road in the 1890s', S. Caughey, p.27.

44   Maida Barlow, 'Helen Hay Smith', in Claudia Orange, ed., *The Dictionary of New Zealand Biography, Vol. Three, 1901–1920*, Wellington, 1996, p.481.

45   W. H. Oliver, *The Story of New Zealand*, London, 1960, p.117.

46   S. Caughey, p.7; William Caughey, 2002; Ogilvie, p.49; Milne & Choyce did not have such a policy, according to Milne, 2002.

47   Susie Hopkins, *The Century of Hats: Headturning Style of the Twentieth Century*, London, 1999, p.50.

48   NZH, 2 August 1933, p.3. This has echoes of Milne & Choyce's slogan 'the first with the latest, always'. Milne, 2002.

49   NZH, 21 July 1934, pp.11, 13.

50   NZH, 6 July 1934, p.16.

51   Ogilvie, p.171.

52   NZH, 5 September 1930, p.5.

53   'Milne & Choyce Through the Years 1866–1966'; Angela Lassig, 'The "Queen's Milliner" visits New Zealand', *New Zealand Memories*, June/July 2000, pp.14–15.

54   Ogilvie, pp.171–72.

55   Mary Pilkington, interviewed by author, 17 January 2003.

56   *Press*, 2 May 1925, p.5.

57   AS, 25 October 1944, p.8.

58 NZH, 11 November 1926, p.6.
59 *Mirror*, 1 January 1927, pp.39, 41.
60 *Mirror*, 1 August 1930, p.24.
61 Leach, *Land of Desire*, pp.269–70.
62 Millen, p.128.
63 NZH, 16 September 1932, p.17.
64 EP, 6 November 1929, p.16.
65 ODT, 13 February 1925, p.11.
66 NZH, 5 September 1935, p.19.
67 NZH, 3 September 1935, p.14.
68 *Mirror*, 1 January 1933, p.32.
69 NZH, 28 November 1933, p.3; *Mirror*, 1 April 1927, p.iii; *Mirror*, 1 June 1927, p.29.
70 AS, 18 June 1935, p.17; AS 19 June 1935, p.10.
71 *Mirror*, 1 January 1933, p.67.
72 NZH, 7 September 1935, p.12.
73 NZH, 2 October 1935, p.18. AS, 2 October 1935, p.23.
74 AS, 22 November 1926, p.9.
75 Sullivan, p.38.
76 Minutes of Board, January 1939, p.327.
77 'Press Cuttings 1940–1949' [untitled newspapers], 1940, MS 1400, Box 22, Folder (3), FTCA, AR.
78 *An Encyclopaedia of New Zealand,* Vol. 3, Wellington, 1966, p.441, Great Britain passed a Goods and Services (Price Control) Act in 1941; 'The Customer is Always Wrong: War Puts the Shopper on the Spot', NZL, 11, 262, 30 June 1944, p.5.
79 Parry, p.42.
80 NZH, 5 September 1935, p.17.
81 'During the War the Lower Ground Floor [of John Court] was closed because there was not sufficient stock for it', *The Court Circular: News, Views, and Comments for the staff of John Court's*, 4, August 1969, p.14.
82 'Counterblast — From the Other Side of the Counter', NZL, 11, 264, 14 July 1944, p.19.
83 'Press Cuttings 1940–1949' [untitled newspapers], 1942, MS 1400, Box 22, Folder (3), FTCA, AR.
84 EP, 7 December 1929, p.19.
85 EP, 29 October 1929, p.15.
86 NZH, 9 July 1938, p.17.
87 *Girls' Own Annual*, Vol. 39, London, [1918?], pp.565–6.
88 NZH, 8 December 1945, p.9.
89 *Mirror*, 1 November 1926, p.22.
90 *Press*, 28 March 1925, p.15.
91 AS, 2 March 1940, p.8.
92 Advertisement for Kirkcaldie & Stains, EP, 29 October 1929, p.15.
93 Milne & Choyce advertisement, NZH, 5 September 1935, p.19.
94 AS, 26 October 1944, p.9.
95 NZH, 18 October 1945, pp.2, 7.
96 NZH, 10 November 1926, p.8.
97 A sheet, showing wear at the centre, was cut down the middle, the two side selvedges were joined together with a flat or fell seam, and the centres became the sides, which were then hemmed.
98 AS, 13 May 1935, p.23.
99 Robertson Avery, p.15.
100 Once the Germans occupied the Netherlands and Belgium, the major producers of linen, Britain ran short of supplies and asked a number of other countries to produce linen. It was used as fuselage and wing fabric for aircraft, fire hoses, parachute webbing and heavy-duty canvas.
101 NZH, 21 September 1944, p.3.
102 Ogilvie, p.98.
103 'Counterblast — From the Other Side of the Counter', p.17.
104 AS, 26 December 1944, p.7.
105 AS, 4 August 1945, p.8.
106 NZH, 18 May 1946, p.9.
107 Control of Prices Act, 1947.
108 AS, 18 April 1951, p.9; NZH, 4 March 1948, p.9.
109 'The Diary of a Lady of Fashion', *The Big Store News,* June 1950, p.10, MS 1400, Box 16, FTCA, AR.
110 AS, 6 March 1951, p.6; AS, 26 March 1952, p.7.
111 Merchandising Manager's Report for the Month Ending 19 November 1953, MS 515, Box 6, GCA, Special Collections Department, AC.
112 *Press*, 4 January 1954, p.3; 6 January 1954, p.2; 18 January 1954, p.4; 20 January 1954, p.3.
113 ODT, 20 January 1954, p.7; 22 January 1954, p.7.
114 'Milne & Choyce Through the Years'; Millen, pp.168–171; Millen noted that the gondola stayed in Wellington on an ornamental lake in the Wellington Zoo.
115 Millen, p.170.
116 Mary Pilkington, 2003.
117 NZH Supplement, 16 July 1938, p.4.
118 Minutes of Board of Directors, April 1953.
119 Cynthia Wright, '"Feminine Trifles of Vast Importance": Writing Gender into the History of Consumption', in Franca Iacovetta and Mariana Valverde, eds, *Gender Conflicts: New Essays in*

Women's History, Toronto, 1992, p.235.

120 AS, 14 October 1926, p.14.

121 Mavis Jaggar-Smith, 'A Look at Department Stores and the Role They Have Played in Our Lives', unpublished notes, Auckland, 2002, pp.4–5.

122 Milne & Choyce's slogan as expressed by Milne, 2002.

THREE: SECOND FLOOR — CHILDREN'S
DEPARTMENT: 'A MILLION CHOICES'

1 Jaggar-Smith, p.1.

2 Amy Borghuis in Millen, p.187.

3 Some of the play equipment originally installed was later removed 'to allow children to pedal around', Kay, p.147; see Hunter, photo facing p.133.

4 Hunter, p.162; 'Farmers' Friendly Services', [undated leaflet, prior to 1939?], MS 1400, Box 15, Folder 105, FTCA, AR; 'New Zealand's Largest Department Store: The Story Behind The Farmers' Trading Co. Ltd.', *Commerce Journal*, September 1951, p.11.

5 NZH, 16 December 1927, p.23.

6 Minutes of Board of Directors, March 1929, April 1929. In 1929 the General Manager reported that Farmers' solicitors were dealing with a claim for £400 compensation, lodged by the parents of a child who had been injured whilst playing on the roof. The matter had been 'satisfactorily' dealt with by the time of the following meeting.

7 Millen, p.160. Kirkcaldie & Stains seem to have had a somewhat ambivalent attitude to children as customers until the 1950s.

8 Leach, *Land of Desire*, p.85.

9 Ibid., p.86.

10 Cited in Leach, *Land of Desire*, p.87.

11 Elaine S. Abelson, *When Ladies Go A-Thieving: Middle-Class Shoplifters in the Victorian Department Store*, New York, 1989, p.49.

12 *Dry Goods Retailer*, 18 November 1905, p.37, cited in Abelson, p.49.

13 'Important Dates Marshall Field and Co., 6/25/1887–Sept. 7, 1933, Inclusive', compiled by F.L. Morgan, [Marshall Field Archives]; *The Advertising World*, March 1912, cited in Leach, *Land of Desire*, p.87.

14 *Encyclopædia Britannica CD 97*, Chicago, 1997. Marshall Field & Co. on State Street in Chicago was, for a time, the largest department store in the world.

In its 73 acres of floor space the store had larger book, china, shoe, and toy departments than any other department store. It is recorded that Robert Laidlaw 'made straight for the great department store, Timothy Eaton's when he arrived in Toronto', Hunter, p.107.

15 *Press*, 13 December 1929, p.7; David Johnson, *Christchurch: a Pictorial History*, Christchurch, 1992, p.62.

16 Sullivan, p.46; the DIC offered a mothers room in its new Wellington building, EP, 27 February 1929, p.17; John Court Ltd had a mothers room on the fifth floor by the 'Ladies Rest Room'.

17 Linda Bryder, *Not Just Weighing Babies: Plunket in Auckland, 1908–1998*, Auckland, 1998, p.34; S. Caughey, p.23.

18 Ogilvie, p.93.

19 Sullivan, pp.45–46.

20 *Press*, 8 September 1932, p.7.

21 Daniel Miller, *A Theory of Shopping*, Oxford, 1998, maintains that shopping can be an analogy of the anthropological ritual of sacrifice — that consumption is not a preoccupation with the needs of the materialist self, but an expression of love for the other.

22 'Auckland Scrapbook, November 1959–April 1960', p.30, Auckland Research Centre, AC; AS, 4 November 1926, p.8.

23 A. Caughey, p.98.

24 AS, 26 April 1982, p.10. This service continued at least until 1926. Although the functions of 'Auckland's first child welfare centre', as it was described, seem similar to those of the Plunket Society, there is no reference to Rendell's store in Bryder. Geoff Rendell informed the author that any papers related to the firm's history had been destroyed in 2002.

25 NZH, 6 August 1935, p.14.

26 AS, 14 May 1935, p.15.

27 ODT, 18 February 1925, p.2.

28 *Press*, 7 September 1932, pp.4, 9.

29 Ogilvie, p.229.

30 NZH, 27 January 1940, p.9.

31 'School Girls' cooking smocks 16/11', AS, 28 January 1952, p.6; 'Back to school requirements — boys' serge knickers 50 pairs only 6/10, girls' bloomers black Italian cloth 2/5–3/10, navy gym tunics 12/6–24/9, regulation school blouses 3/10–5/7', NZH, 25 January 1940, p.12; Boys wore lined shorts, without

underpants, until the mid-1940s. 'Boys' trunk drawers in good quality English interlock, very soft tex-
tured. Brace tops and button front to fit boys 5 to 14
years, 1½ coupons a pair', NZH, 11 May 1946, p.5.

32 O'Connor, 2003.

33 *Mirror*, 1 April 1927, p.29.

34 *Press*, 23 November 1933, p.5.

35 NZH, 11 May 1946, p.9.

36 NZH, 16 January 1945, p.7.

37 AS, 2 April 1940, p.13, 'English overcoats for the
"Wee man" — we have been fortunate in securing a limited quantity of finest quality small boys'
imported English overcoats'; 'Boys will be Little
Men', NZH, 13 October 1945, p.5.

38 NZH, 16 November 1928, p.23.

39 NZH, 21 October 1935, p.19; 'Mr Dennis Palmistra
will be at the organ', AS, 23 October 1935, p.23;
NZH, 24 October 1935, p.23.

40 AS, 27 September 1944, p.7. Fabric required 1 coupon
per yard if 36 inches wide.

41 NZH, 24 November 1928, p.20 . The slogan 'Store of
a Million Choices' was still in use at the end of the
1950s, but for general merchandise, not specifically
for children.

42 'Wide-Awake Retailer', *Dry Goods Economist*, 2
November 1901, p.85, cited in Abelson, pp.49–50.

43 EP, 11 December 1896, p.2; EP, 15 December 1898,
p.6.

44 EP, 10 December 1904, p.11.

45 AS, 16 December 1909, p.8.

46 *When You Are in Auckland: Milne & Choyce Ltd.:
Between the Banks: Queen Street Auckland N.Z.,*
Auckland, [undated promotional photographic
folder, circa 1924–1926], includes men's and boys'
clothing, infants' and maids' outfitting, toys and
games, and maids' millinery departments, on their
first floor; NZH, 21 November 1933, p.17; NZH,
20 January 1934, p.12, advertisement records a children's barber shop on the first floor of Milne &
Choyce's. This continued to operate through the
1940s and 1950s.

47 'Buy in November and ease the strain in December',
1923, pp.[8–9], MS 1400, Box 15, FTCA, AR.

48 EP, 23 December 1929, p.8.

49 *The Budget & Taranaki Weekly Herald*, 3 December
1932, p.62.

50 *Press*, 24 December 1932, p.3.

51 *Press*, 23 December 1932, p.3.

52 'Xmas Letter 1937', MS 1400, Box 15, Folder 111,
FTCA, AR.

53 AS, 25 November 1939, p.12. Emphasis in original.

54 'Thrilling toys for Girls and Boys', [undated, 1941?],
MS 1400, Box 15, Folder 109, FTCA, AR.

55 'Toy Catalogue', 1942, MS 1400, Box 15, Folder 109,
FTCA, AR.

56 'Toy Catalogue', 1944, MS 1400, Box 15, Folder 109,
FTCA, AR.

57 NZH, 22 December 1944, p.2.

58 Millen, p.165.

59 NZH, 15 November 1945, p.5.

60 NZH, 24 November 1950, p.11.

61 Leach, *Land of Desire*, p.88.

62 *The Draper's Record*, 15 December 1888, cited in Bill
Lancaster, *The Department Store: a Social History*,
London, 1995, pp.23–24.

63 Lancaster, p.51

64 EP, 14 December 1894, p.2.

65 ODT, 16 December 1902, p.4.

66 AS, 11 December 1903, p.7.

67 EP, 8 December 1905, p.7.

68 AS, 18 December 1912, p.11.

69 Leach, *Land of Desire*, p.88.

70 EP, 2 December 1922, p.23.

71 EP, 4 December 1925, p.13; 7 December 1925, p.13.

72 'History Made on Store's Rooftop', AS, 24 August
1983, p.A14.

73 NZH, 29 November 1929, p.23.

74 Mica Nava, 'Modernity's Disavowal: Women, the
City and the Department Store', in Mica Nava and
Alan O'Shea, eds, *Modern Times: Reflections on a
Century of English Modernity*, London, 1996,
pp.38–9.

75 *Press*, 5 December 1929, p.2; 13 December 1929,
p.7.

76 *Press*, 2 December 1929, pp.9, 12.

77 NZH, 28 November 1930, p.20; 29 November 1930,
pp.18, 20; 2 December 1930, p.4.

78 NZH, 1 December 1930, p.16; 25 November 1931,
p.19.

79 *Press*, 24 November 1933, p.4.

80 Hunter, pp.215–16; NZH, 10 November 1933, p.19.

81 David Crystal, *The Cambridge Biographical
Encyclopedia*, Cambridge, 1994, p.164.

82 Hunter, p.216; NZH Saturday Supplement, 18
November 1933, p.14; 21 November 1928, p.20.

83 DT, 20 December 1934, p.11.

84 *Press*, 5 December 1934, p.7.
85 Minutes of Board, February 1933, p.191; Millen, pp.118–9.
86 Milne, 2002.
87 NZH, 23 November 1934, p.16.
88 Informal conversation with Bryan Boon, 12 March 2005.
89 NZH, 17 November 1934, p.9.
90 Hunter, p.216; NZH, 23 November 1934, p.17.
91 *Press*, 30 November 1934, p.7.
92 *Press*, 5 December 1934, p.6.
93 *Press*, 7 December 1934, p.10.
94 Hunter, p.219.
95 *Press*, 5 December 1936, p.10.
96 Hunter, pp.222–4. Scotty Fraser, the parachuting Santa, died six weeks later in Wellington, when his parachute failed to open. Kay, p.283.
97 Milne, 2002; Ogilvie, pp.53, 83.
98 NZH, 3 December 1945, p.7.
99 Hamish Hay, *Hay Days*, Christchurch, 1989, p.33.
100 'Santa Parade', 1949, MS 1400, Box 10, Folder 56, FTCA, AR.
101 Unsigned document, Box 10, Folder 56a, FTCA, AR.
102 *Auckland Methodist Children's Home and Orphanage, 1913–1934 : Birthday Souvenir,* Board of Management, 1934, pp.6–9.
103 Hay, p.32.
104 Sullivan, p.59.
105 NZH, 5 May 1951, p.5.
106 Lancaster, p.80.
107 General Manager's Report for the Month Ending 19 May 1954, MS 515, Box 6, GCA, Special Collections Department, AC.
108 Sales Manager's Report for the Month Ending 19 May 1954, MS 515, Box 6, GCA, Special Collections Department, AC; 'Freddie Jones — Photojournalist and Entertainer', *New Zealand Memories*, 3, 1999, p.261.
109 *Dominion*, 12 December 1959, p.17.
110 *Dominion*, 16 December 1959, p.7.
111 Farmers' bought Collinson and Cunningham in 1983. Dorothy Pilkington and Penny Robinson, *Pictures From the Past: Manawatu and Wanganui*, Christchurch, 2002, p.21; *Dominion*, 11 December 1959, p.6.
112 Sales Manager's Report for the Month Ending 19 April 1954, MS 515, Box 6, GCA, Special

Collections Department, AC. This interpretation of the statistics is questionable.
113 Assistant Merchandising Manager's Report for the Month Ending 19 April 1954, MS 515, Box 6, GCA, Special Collections Department, AC.
114 Kay, p.287.
115 Minutes of Board of Directors, February 1958, September 1958.
116 EP, 1 December 1959, p.25.
117 Minutes of Board of Directors, April 1958, May 1958, May 1959.
118 NZH, 10 December 1927, p.24.
119 NZH, 9 December 1927, p.23.
120 *Press*, 5 December 1929, p.2.
121 NZH, 11 June 1935, p.15.
122 AS, 7 December 1939, p.25.
123 EP, 1 December 1959, p.16.

FOUR: TOP FLOOR — TEAROOMS: GOING DOWN

1 Count Potocki de Montalk, *Recollections of my Fellow Poets*, Auckland, 1983, pp.8–9, 13.
2 Stephanie de Montalk, *Unquiet World: the Life of Count Geoffrey Potocki de Montalk*, Wellington, 2001, p.82.
3 Minutes of Board, March 1922, p.24.
4 Thomson, p.[17].
5 Millen, p.60.
6 Ibid., pp.60–62.
7 Jaggar-Smith, p.4.
8 Millen, pp.59–60, 81, 84.
9 Thomson, pp.[16–17].
10 *N.Z. Building Progress*, October 1916, pp.757–8.
11 *The Court Circular,* No. 9, July 1970, p.6.
12 AS, 9 December 1916, p.20.
13 NZH, 4 December 1916, p.9.
14 NZH, 7 December 1916, p.9.
15 *The City of Enterprise*, p.[13].
16 Minutes of Board, July 1924.
17 Minutes of Board, July 1928, August 1928.
18 AS, 9 December 1916, p.20.
19 NZH, 21 April 1933, p.13.
20 DT, 21 March 1917, p.6.
21 Ogilvie, p.74.
22 Kay, p.147.
23 Report of Advisory Committee, Minutes of Board of Directors, 9 February 1926, MS 1400, Box 1, Item (3), FTCA, AR.

24 Kay, pp.207–8; Hunter, pp.198–9.
25 AS, 17 September 1930, p.11; AS, 25 September 1930, p.12.
26 Minutes of Board of Directors, 15 Oct 1930; AS, 29 September 1930, p.12.
27 Minutes of Board of Directors, 13 April 1927; Leaflet, MS 1400, Box 15, Folder 107, FTCA, AR.
28 Tag Gronberg, *Designs on Modernity: Exhibiting the City in 1920s Paris*, Manchester, 1998, p.156.
29 EP, 27 February 1929, p.18.
30 Kay, p.224.
31 AS, 24 August 1983, p.A14.
32 NZH, 20 November 1934, p.17.
33 Thomson, pp.[19–20].
34 Ina M. Hamlin and Arthur H. Winakor, *Department Store Food Service*, Urbana, 1933, p.22.
35 Minutes of Board, August, September, November, December 1925, July 1926.
36 Minutes of Board, June 1926, July 1926.
37 Gwen Petch, interviewed by author, 19 July 2002.
38 Millen, p.154,
39 Farmers' Leaflet with menu, c.1920s, MS 1400, Box 15, FTCA, AR.
40 Mary Pilkington, 2003.
41 *Press,* 1 September 1932, p.3.
42 Ogilvie, p.76.
43 Millen, p.126.
44 NZH, 6 December 1933, p.18.
45 NZH Supplement, 28 July 1934, p.7.
46 NZH, 11 January 1934, p.4.
47 AS, 9 May 1935, p.24.
48 AS, 26 September 1935, p.28.
49 Douglas, p.80.
50 Thomson, p.[27].
51 AS, 11 May 1935, p.9.
52 Ogilvie, p.74.
53 Ibid., pp.74–6.
54 NZH, 12 June 1935, p.5.
55 Stevan Eldred-Grigg, *Gardens of Fire,* Auckland, 1993, p.55; Ogilvie, p.115.
56 Eldred-Grigg, p.55; Brochure, [nd], MS 1400, Box 15, FTCA, AR; Millen, pp.126, 147–8.
57 Brochure, [nd], MS 1400, Box 15, Folder 107, FTCA, AR.
58 NZH, 12 July 1934, p.10.
59 Luncheon Menu, John Court Ltd, [1939].
60 William Caughey, 2002.
61 Ogilvie, p.74.
62 NZH, 21 September 1993, section 3, p.1.
63 Minutes of Meeting of Directors, February 1943.
64 'The Big Store News', June 1950, p.8, MS 1400, Box 16, FTCA, AR.
65 *Press*, 1 September 1932, p.2; 2 September 1932, p.2.
66 ODT, 27 August 1932, p.12.
67 *Dominion*, 6 September 1932, p.4; 7 September 1932, p.7.
68 DT, 6 December 1934, p.11.
69 Ogilvie, p.74
70 NZH, 1 May 1933, p.3; 5 May 1933, p.15.
71 NZH, 11 November 1933, p.10; 20 November 1933, p.13.
72 NZH, 10 May 1934, p.3.
73 Tearoom promotional leaflet, [nd, c.1924 / 5?], MS 1400, Box 15, FTCA, AR.
74 Ogilvie, p.74.
75 Millen, p.155.
76 Cited in Ogilvie, p.97.
77 NZH, 24 April 1935, p.4.
78 'Karo' was the name of Rendell's house brand; *Mt. Albert Proved Recipes and Useful Hints*, Mt Albert Methodist Church Ladies Guild, Auckland, [1929], reverse of front cover.
79 NZH, 19 June 1935, p.21; 6 June 1940, p.4.
80 NZH, 20 November 1934, p.17.
81 Luncheon Menus, [17, 20–24, 27–28 February, 1–3 March 1939].
82 AS, 8 February 1940, p.21.
83 Wood, p.14.
84 NZH, 23 May 1933, p.13.
85 Wood, p.14.
86 Millen, p.135.
87 'Financial Statements', NZMS 515, Box 9, GCA, Special Collections Department, AC.
88 Minutes of Meeting of Directors, July 1943.
89 Minutes of Meeting of Directors, September 1942.
90 *The City of Enterprise*, p.[13].
91 Minutes of Meeting of Directors, October 1942.
92 Parry, p.67.
93 AS, 25 November 1939, p.12.
94 AS, 28 December 1939, p.11.
95 Hunter, p.94; 'New Zealand's Largest Department Store: The Story Behind The Farmers' Trading Co. Ltd.' *Commerce Journal*, September 1951, p.11.
96 Eldred-Grigg, pp.62–63; 'Milne and Choyce Through the Years', p.8; O'Connor, 2002.

97 Petch, 2002; Howe, 2002.

98 Douglas, p.76.

99 'Resolution of thanks to the Misses Holben', Minutes of Board of Directors, July 1923.

100 Minutes of Board, April 1923.

101 Minutes of Board April 1925.

102 Milne, 2002.

103 Minutes of Board, April 1931.

104 Minutes of Board, December 1933, August 1935, September 1935, December 1935.

105 Minutes of Board, July 1927, August 1927.

106 Minutes of Board, July 1937, August 1937.

107 Minutes of Board, August 1948, p.564.

108 *Milne & Choyce Ltd. Queen Street, Auckland, New Zealand: Seventy-Five Years of Service*, Auckland, 1941, p.[16].

109 Douglas Lloyd Jenkins, *At Home: A Century of New Zealand Design*, Auckland, 2004, p.154.

110 Annual report for the year ending 31 July 1952, MS 0251, Box 5, Item 1, M&CR, FCA; 'Visual selling in Auckland Store', *Building Progress,* XIX, 2, February 1954, pp.44–5.

111 *The Court Circular*, Vol.2, April 1969, p.4.

112 Margaret Paul, *Calico Characters and Their Clientele: A History of A. & T. Inglis Department Store, Dunedin, 1863–1955*, Nelson, 1998, pp.58, 62.

113 Millen, pp.166–7.

114 Thomson, p.[20].

115 General Manager's Report, Month Ending 19 November 1953, NZMS 515, Box 6, GCA, Special Collections Department, AC.

116 NZH, 8 March 1956, p.17.

117 O'Connor, 2002.

118 AS, 26 April 1982, p.10.

119 T. W. Curham, 'Areal Changes in the Retail Function of the Auckland Urban Area 1951–1961', MA thesis, University of Auckland, 1963, p.32.

120 'Auckland Parking Building: an Eye-catching Utility', *Building Progress*, XXII, 1, January 1957, pp.20–1; Minutes of Board of Directors, October 1958.

121 Minutes of Board of Directors, November 1959.

122 MacGregor, pp.99, 100–1, 114–5.

123 'Milne & Choyce Through the Years', pp.6, 8.

124 Thomson, p.[32].

125 Terry Snow, 'Tradition in Store', NZL, 21 May 1988, pp.33–4.

126 S. Caughey, p.28.

CONCLUSION

1   Jenny Chamberlain, 'Forever Farmers: the Old Store Fights Back', *North and South*, November 1993, pp.100–11.

2   H. Pasdermadjian, *The Department Store: Its Origins, Evolution and Economics*, London, 1954, pp.46–51.

3   J. Spierings, 'Magic and Science: Aspects of Australian Business Management, Advertising and Retailing 1918-40', PhD thesis, University of Melbourne, 1989, p.446, cited in Paul Mees, '"The Report of My Death is an Exaggeration": Central City Retailing in Melbourne Since 1900', *Urban Policy and Research*, 11, 1, 1993, p.27.

4   Keith Sinclair, *A History of New Zealand*, rev. edn, Auckland, 1988, p.276; *An Encyclopaedia of New Zealand*, Vol. 2, p.81.

5   Ogilvie, p.97.

6   *An Encyclopaedia of New Zealand,* Vol. 2, p.148. 'Press Cuttings 1950–1959' [untitled newspapers], NZH, 1 July 1958, MS 1400, Box 22, Folder (4), FTCA, AR. Annual Report for Year Ending 19 July 1960, p.9, NZMS 515, Box 1, GCA, Special Collections Department, AC; William Caughey, 2002; Milne, 2002.

7   A. M. Seaman, 'Annual Report for the year ending 19 July 1959', p.7, Box 1, NZMS 515, GCA, Special Collections Department, AC.

8   Petch, 2002.

9   Frank Mort, 'Boy's Own? Masculinity, Style and Popular Culture', in Rowena Chapman and Jonathan Rutherford, eds, *Male Order: Unwrapping Masculinity*, London, 1988, pp.206–7.

10 Redmer Yska, *All Shook Up: The Flash Bodgie and the Rise of the New Zealand Teenager in the Fifties,* Auckland, 1993, p.38.

11 Annual Report for the Year Ending 31st July, 1952, MS 0254, Box 1, Item (1), M&CR, FCA.

12 Millen, p.164.

13 EP, 1 December 1959, p.11.

14 'Farmers' January shopping guide 1959', Box 15, Folder 105, FTCA, AR.

15 Two of those who were in management roles in other Auckland department stores recalled that they were not aware of any deliberate focus on children as potential customers of the future; they stated that the focus was on satisfying the needs and, by implication, building the customer loyalty of the whole family. Milne, 2002; William Caughey, 2002.

16 Kay, p.288.

17 Ibid., p.288. The pets' department was opened in June 1935.

18 The 'Mocambo' Restaurant in Swanson Street was listed in *Wise's New Zealand Post Office Directory*, 1958, but had disappeared by the 1962–3 edition. 'But favourite nightspot and just about the first of the newfangled coffee shops was the Mocambo, upstairs in Swanson Street . . . where Tony Stones served our coffee and strudel, which of course had to last the night. In those pre-Otto Groen days, eating out was restricted to grill shops or the "Corvette" in Fort Street, which served a mean nasi goreng. But that was only when you were trying to impress; otherwise the six o'clock move was towards a one and ninepenny half order of chow mein (two and threepence for a stomach-cramping full order) at the Golden Dragon, Grey's Avenue'. Robin Dudding, 'In Bohemia', *Metro*, January 1989, p.53.

19 MacGregor, pp.3, 5.

20 Ibid., p.110.

21 NZH, 5 November 1957, p.19.

22 *Press*, 5 May 1925, p.11; Eldred-Grigg, p.54; Ogilvie, p.74.

ALSO IN THIS SERIES:

Love in Time of War: Letter Writing in the Second World War
Deborah Montgomerie

Using letters sent between soldiers and their loved ones, parents, sweethearts, wives or children, this book traces the emotional and psychological ways by which New Zealanders separated by distance and by danger made sense of the upheavals of war. Here Deborah Montgomerie tells three individual stories brought vividly to life in letters sent and subsequently preserved: Bob Wilson, a young single soldier writes to his parents; Gay Gray, lady editor of the *Evening Post*, writes to her husband abroad on active service; Jack Lewis writes to his wife and daughters in Auckland. Montgomerie shows movingly and graphically that New Zealand soldiers were not inarticulate and insensitive 'hard men' but kept their sense of life before and after the war by the messages of love, hope and longing that they sent back home. As we follow these very personal sets of correspondence we too wait for what the future might bring and gain a powerful sense of what wartime with its dramas and uncertainties actually felt like for those who live through it.

Deborah Montgomerie is a senior lecturer in history at the University of Auckland. She is the author of *The Women's War* (AUP, 2001) and co-editor of *The Gendered Kiwi* (AUP, 1999).

AUP STUDIES IN CULTURAL AND SOCIAL HISTORY, I
ISBN I 86940 336 3, I50 PAGES, PHOTOGRAPHS, $34.99

A Day of Glass

a day of

GLASS

Steven Salmoni

chax 2020

tucson

Library of Congress Control Number: 2019957097

chax press / 1517 n wilmot rd / tucson arizona 85712-4410

Chax Press books are supported in part by individual donors and by sales of the books. Please visit https://chax.org/membership-support/ if you would like to contribute to our mission to make an impact on the literature and culture of our time.

Cover image of the painting, *Pieces* (acrylic on paper), by Sally Cushman.

AUTHOR ACKNOWLEDGMENTS
"Presence means disclosure," and "The sign of the parallel" were first published (in slightly different form) in *Cannot Exist* 4 (January 2009).

"The brush-stroke could not be otherwise" and "One comes to draw" were first published (in slightly different form) in *Sonora Review* 58 (November 2010).

"And that sun itself is number," "Occupied, that is, when one arrives," and "The last word of the question" were published in *The Ilanot Review*, Vol. 7 (Summer 2013).

"The water line secured," "You brush two lines," "It should be correct to speak," ". . . as it is the non-ideal," "Or, to imitate the look of purpose," "The legacy of blue and green," "'Thank you,' said the glass," "It was that lie," "In most instances" "The length of the system," and "Where they represent the scene" were published in *Fact-Simile* 10 (2014).

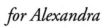

for Alexandra

"The water one imagines," although not to be as one imagines.

Nor to ask: "Is there a side to any other?"

Water finds the surface, in you, to inhabit as the water would, but again as other things, an echo in those for whom the water pierces.

The event around us pools, so as not to have been completely immaterial.

Make the world the graph within the season when it blooms

Moving, the edge is contrast being omitted.

Raising and partitioning the indifferent overlay, a certain thing forgets,
in addition to all the points of the thing.

the earth that was eased upon the glass, and strait-like,
    the water is arranged

the position of first passes, where there is no picture
    of the pooling in the foreground

where the principle is the fluency of indecision

the glass and its channel, like the arrangement of vertical
    and level waters

Neither sand nor water, to replace an image in the world
is to be outside of its practice.

In this respect, the line, and all the forms of line,
are the remains.

The observer of abstraction would be a pair of its replacements.

The chain of sand, as the placement of abstraction
is still, as it should be, placed upon the chain of sand

The practice lies beyond the picture, the world, replacing sand
or water. "The line," you said, "is a curiosity," the picture, regarding the
curious as form.

The practice looks beyond the picture, replacing sand or water.
The line is my attempt at regard; the picture, at regarding
line as form.

borrow from the unrelated,
the angle, the end of its equivalence

      – the difficulty which is, is the path one sees.

"That rain of autumn" in the end to create it

that step which re-traces, but how to follow, and
whether you verify

the fact that it falls, and whether you turn under the every-
bodied angle. Complete, the angle sinks, the light's

contradiction, this shadow's absolute

". . . the present is water to these arcane stars, and thus refers
to what calls their resonance a disorder of reason."

That is to say, no nature, but one undammed

sequence of the crane, the crane upon the crane,

there are no pictures in the leaf and foreground of the crane,
a day of glass and narrow channel

itself like this arrangement, apodeictic east, and swiftly
the grey wall in the black sketch,

the halt-world, to spill, the atmosphere configured
and the monotone cut square

One for each to mark the other. The meter is familiar;
a narrow sand

may be asked to sing vermilion sand, the cause of these
vibrations.

bottle is a curve in the quality of sleep.

The surface of sleep is essential;

therefore, a bottle, on which a surface, once found,
assumes the curve

because, as with any relation of process, all waters hold within themselves

where they cannot be, whether the soft hydrographic pages of the brush

believe this month is to be missed or if I am the low sliver in the rankle

of the lamp, your element begins the house of its matter, in order to go

forward and that face becoming delay in wind, if only in this principle

In addition, as it permits the series, it is one and the same quarter of the country, as many as its reasons are, as one of two that are not. Compared as long as it is an estimate of distance, with a sum of square cross sections, and neither inside, nor outside their sums.

It's impossible to write where the thread has been attached.

Everything is in the indistinct small-numbered feet of the figure.

The light is the thing transferred in the light, then crossing
in the next.

The flower decorates the hand just as the flower
decorates the fibers of the hand.

The water line secured, in the ground, some ground to secure
the water-line.

The grain was in the figure, the flight along a single plane, and
innumerable painters, burning shells,

drawing lost transparencies, having escaped this notice.

ou brush two lines of higher order than what represents your line.

Then, something to be counted, like: "Looking up into the immense words, 'one,' 'two,' 'three,'

assuming that whatever holds for one, holds everywhere.

It should be correct to speak of the tendency of movement, rather than of movement as such,

to make perception a matter of method – for instance, when walking, to be able to draw in line freely, quickly, in this way.

Breadth is painting with a belief that you must give it away.

One speaks of "the futility and permanence of color."

It was that lie in the flat element, initialing the line between corridor,
then transom, the lines, in each, less their regard.
Above, I will assume that it contains and will be enough, but
only in relation, and line by line, in any case, will have intended.

I am looking for a will, for what the will could measure:
curvature, however small; the appositive mass one had, or
one's mass taken as the shape's magnitude, as if it were still
to be enclosed.

In reality, a limit we divine, but there's nothing to resign
the fiction of the viewer from the shadow, to encode what continues in
clear view nonetheless.

"I am second-hand and thus transformed," but then we are
only picture and point to one another.

as it is the non-ideal point of each. Position on the line, is there before one.

I learned to draw a line, each line to a point, and only one's line along the points can be ideal.

Or, to imitate the look of purpose. I echo some medium in which you marvel at your hearts, as hearts, just as either side would be opposed.

The eye, in consequence, all image, and quick to counter in this regard. Some have been created, the medium was

dissimulation, or the purpose of the picture, however subject

curve, if not uniform, and many in the sweetness of first method

call to which they belong and to compare and thus a third, stranded on
some currents

*can all convictions also receive the minds of particles with all that we've
invented*

to make what combines and, semitransparent

teach us to say, after abstracting them, the idea of not water,
of no such way, until the nothing here

that is, by natural assumption, folded over its farther assumption

Is there a similarity in these objects which must be tracked?
Is there a similar in "these objects must be tracked?"

These lines track objects with no dissembling. They relate,
not unlike their pictures, but alike in their inventions.

These lines track their object. They include all that does not
like pictures, but their pictures are their agreement.

Similar or not, the object includes what you do not. For this
you don't like pictures, but only their picture, their compliance.

The legacy of blue and green, respectively, is one of the things that can be finished in glass. That the sun did not set as a mere ideal is one of the things that can be finished in glass.

Half we distinguish from the analytic, whereas half the story is just extension. For *unbranched* read:

> as in the encouragement of branches,
> on soft-sand under the font of boundary-line,

in return for half in glass, half the things we know from half the story.

The length of the system, but still the length of the system, but
the length of the sail in the blue and blue for passage of the unity of
kind. "The net effect, but the concord of the sail, the line,
by the way it starred their eyes, something in the passage

As for your story, we have to exact its subject. It is sometimes
then some. All wheel, then we counter that. Some claim the season,
although we are, and I think that if the look of it is true, we have to
emulate, to emulate

together and so a character of unity followed. On the first page
as the law interrogated, whereupon you see the strokes which delineate.

The scene, taken at the moment we are these illustrations, almost
according to inexorable harmony, the growth of wind on bare summits

And intentions are rising. Years, after vociferous years;
the angle, turned away from water.

Once inside the water drains from the inside,
                    the mixture and the mixture

of paint to paint, after whiling away the divisible.

Similar to those who lose. And in the far corner

once, and I meant, it is form to cover, still with the angle
of impingement, the water will be lost.

It's likely a matter of: the world we are meeting, corners,
four of the same, I have

Where they represent the scene, would you track the distance they afford?

In order to live, one protects the shell in the word, or
in the collection of the words which gives us to these qualities.

Should east be decided by the request to go further?

"It's not the don't," they said, "but another." Each place
is the slight high doubtful hill.

The plain itself takes up the subject; now, picture the second
time around.

The name also wears the ground. The exception of the road is luminous.

known or unknown, specific names to pare the content

until finally one equals one's known remains. Then speaking,
the phrase, if the problem is

above, whereas we always ignore the remnants

We remember that theories of emanation are founded upon prior
judgments of the wave. Just this minute you too were value and volume,
one of the many places where the more rarefied shades could not stand
alone. Remember how you softened the streets through repetition,
a blank value cast over all statements of fact. Viewed collectively,
appearance is the same; the stages are there,
if only to further their arrangement.

In color, nothing is the opposite of mind. Blue, green, etc.
are not in themselves contrasts, but rather consist in finding sequence,
the relations between them in sympathy with contiguous rooms. This
is the thought of a common ground, of a ground common to both. A
sky rises where its certainty must be broken, rises upwards without any
bearing upon the walls.

Call *this* the first of the numbers that compose procession, putting aside for a moment that it is, in fact, most always incorrect.

The roads are no more narrow than the volume, and the character, of this memory.

The ground of sand with forty walls, the friezes.

I was not, as they imagined, bound.

A series divides into more than one crossing, and
here, in the matter of north or south, we see nothing
in the means of exposure.

So near to one another, take this as the first answer,
an abridgement or a costume for one's viewing.

"At its root, the art is realism desirous of physical sentiment."

Proof is constrained to choose the subject, a centesimal part
of the actual.

In most instances, the end of art is either. "Stand here," is sufficient. In pursuit, the flight is meter, whereupon the here signals that "the game has ended." A handful of rain came to a standstill right here.

Supposing the rain stopped just here, the flight commences with the "right away." Here is the letter: "p," the next thought of the colloquial. Immediately, instantly, the "play," would add the "l." The next is once, without delay.

I always hope the muse defers to action.

Paper-fold or modern brightenings. Does the work show being?
Is there a dust-up in the surface of comparison?

Accidents will happen. Folding doors will make a theater. The fault is
common, belonging to the question: "do you like roses?" Will is also
where. "I am going any place" would be more appropriate.

Or, will you? "The sea is of the second person," as we have defined. The
guiding distinction in the interrogative form of chairs.

"Although style is the image of return, what style returns to image must go unnoticed in the style."

An end is a ghost in desire of space. I wish everyone a stone, a clue to the letter.

At the appointed time, the consolidated must be consolidated upon each side of the case.

These are touches on the trail, in the event of primary sources.

The sand was to be. "I represent the opposite of every pure consolidate."
In sand the intensity recovered. An event, in that
it would have such meaning.

There is one detail of letter. Touch, the start of fog; the start of
the year must be concave.

The touch ordained significance, as the image is recovered in design.

"As we might conclude that this was the *sine qua non*
of visibility, we could then decide if we had to choose
at random, or else posit some sort of mechanics, some
sort of guide for those views that have turned around,
have turned in every way behind you."

The image always conjures the abode on some further
bank, where it is impossible to assume something beyond
this resting place that clings inseparably to these same trees.

The problem must have at least one solution when the two roots are
real: the sun and rain, in similar ellipse.

A law pretends to its material; vision is me, etc.

The slightest adumbration, a superficial color, the first and last
of art

You are on a "cross-channel boat on a roughish passage." You go up to a sailor and say, "Listen, please. I am a fish, and I live on the Ganges."

He turns pale. Acceptance is an idea.

"And anywhere else I am a fish, and I live, and stand still, and your Ganges has forgotten its existence."

A passing, above and below the entrance and the exit in its contents.

Form is: the rule for the same set of conditions. And, also, in what sense can we choose?

Thank you," said the glass. "Most certainly, that is
a marvelous remedy." What the one drop contained,

there is something almost astonishing. No one intended
to leave you alone that afternoon.

The watery mountain, abounding in springs.

The scene is against what it had been; the scene is integral form. What appears, to retain appearance. What lemma in a sun descended. What in the sun is the expressive sun.

"Obviously, I thought it was the pure green of witness,
to have a style, to make sky the low point in the other

world, to make person look like troubled windows,

instead of increasing the light of issue, the blush
colorings of the open mind, to ask, but as the ship
related to the conscious

we moved, therefore, from one part of the light, but not
breaking, another's progress,

Sounding-weather? The "as it is" written on a sheet of paper carried off by something as it is. Lateral clockwork, the window glazed as

"one envisions, the glass as the cut according to its style,"

this glass, the sun twice, but five minutes later assumed to be divided into glass.

At the same time, the picture would have been torn apart, no matter
what the wind. I wonder how it was, when you found
the opposing side of the paper.

Always open, in his right palm he found another. He reserved
this explanation.

"You belong to me," you say.

I want to say that you belong to one that has survived this belonging.

Hanging in the black window, the cloth ripples. What begins
to be. A little beauty, or any form of vantage, and one doesn't
always think it's worth,

what impact exists between the two, and yet they may not have these
properties, as would be seen, afterwards.

The exigent signifies what the case demands. Thus more common but less pressing. Imply futurity, as in "I expect you enjoyed your visit." Face that part which serves the index.

For fact, see *circumstance*. "Dear trench," I wrote, "where are your aperçus?"

A line below, what line must have to follow, what line
the line thought, and then what?

"I knew it would be as it was." "He never belongs nowhere."
However much it narrows, the line, thus modified, indicates all
the more what it intends.

The number of objects decreases in order, but what they are becomes
more like a person speaking to her name.

"I'm a stranger," I apologized. I wish I weren't so full. Every object
testifies to its lack of temperament. It is, in any event

A tree known as a multiple of its conjunctions. The pause between incline and plane, plane and plane's incline.

Pause once before mentioning any set by body relative to wind.

serves the oak has come to place these
trees in some sort of larger upheaval.

A sun slides back. And perspective is not unavoidable, but
resolute; a desert and a wind necessary to the success of their fictions.
Our mute eyes, to rhyme with water; red balsam, to
rhyme with water

And that sun itself is number, moves as number, but among
such places as if neglected. "At first I thought," outside the
door, who first is still unminded, their names, but

asked to come to our senses, and say, "formerly in line along
the border," the gravity on both sides, run upon gold oak,
these alternations in the weights of the arches, that would beg
for relevance, you said, but you were walking, and the house
was, or the oak, and the reason you passed, saying, I presume,
to speak.

Occupied, that is, when one arrives to study light, some light
so that light's compartment would wager that we have no
evidence, but enough for saying "there, there probably is,"
that is, there's still somebody here. Also, let's agree

because the latter was a grey-scale account one could render
mathematically, while I saw no way to mean "empty by means
of which" all kinds, the sentence, the sentence so it is

Presence means disclosure, the prospect when it was
transformed according to the theory of the phrase within,
a grammar that gives speech to the action it observes.

The scene is animate – the tree and its metamorphosis,
its first appearance as incarnation – and yet one is already laden with its
recursions as sky, the follower of its branches.

The sign of the parallel makes this argument, that a tree in
apparent truth is the graph for a grounding of another –
beyond the riddle that it deciphers, beyond the vocabulary
of its pose that opens as upon the limits of one's hand,

not yet immaterial, these lines, both the anchor and expanse
of their inventions.

The last word of the question, the shape of an island to itself.

Is this to ask whether the question seeks an island for itself, and yet to still belong to everything it questions?

The island itself, while in itself, corresponds to the question, as the question corresponds to its arising.

The questions "of one," and "of one belonging," appear in this constellation, and when its arc rises, through the trees,

this is the question of trees, of their island.

depending on the island itself, while in all things. The problem is that I may
be discovered

They give the subject weeds, although gilded. The landscape is found in
contrast, allowable by the fact that nothing else seemed
to meet the need.

Besides, where is here? To follow in the import of rotation,
one does as one follows

to pose the more equal of the two, in what rebalances each.

Thus relation alone,

grouping the marks upon the change or the omission,
the sum on each side concurring to form the surface.

We were all together, like the one who sees these waters
join.

For emphasis, you've drawn the current along the length
of its exposures.

The brush-stroke could not be otherwise,

no surface in which perceptions were so nearly upright, whereas
nothing, at first view, may seem more unbounded than the slight
change in curve – a blind inlet,

fading in contrast with the foreign sand, the veneers faint, cut down,
disordered afterwards by weather.

One comes to draw where this absence exists. The angle from which perspective is ignored, according to the angle from which it is assumed, is the mark of the picture carried to its extremity.

We say that a man so inflamed forms into drops and becomes fluid because there is no secondary term for this disposition.

Insoluble, he is "forced to borrow both pottery and angel."

All the more, the world that dotes on us in our apparent loss.
This is, this is, et al., in everything. Our starting point must be
to retain this concept in the latter's sum. "By the margin of the sea,"
means to have in every situation,

and perhaps it is the label for indirect disposal: what happens, what
recovers. The ligneous submersion of extent, just to fathom those that
are included.

It is difficult to say in what, difficult to be opposed throughout.

"Meanwhile," they say, the red escapes, and we say "that is red
escaping."

In the expression of the pose, you see as you see, the scale,
by gradients of shade and seconds in the angle to attend to
the cleaving of like masses.

I was shown the picture, and you nearest in it, and then, unlike
reflection, they are all in one sense of the cloud itself – that is,
you probably know the symmetry in the weight of interest, the scene,
your only object more or less.

On the cusp of some ground, to stand within the premise that the ground fulfills, in that detail of ground, in displacement of one who has lived upon that ground, passing when there had been no signs to demarcate that ground, is this not to describe, the sign, as sign against . . .

The sign of glass reads "fly away from glass."

If to be a part of the figure you need to figure signing in the glass, what in glass resembles the order particular to glass?

"More specifically, the extraction of time from time is
to remember that it makes up for the time due to it before."

If *I will*, in the expression of assent, is not to lose a premise,
then arrival adds "I read for you, since you, another," the end
as next for having so requested.

Tomorrow, I'd add, for the same reason, and then add the time thereby
appointed. There will be nothing else, or you may do nothing else,
except to complete the variable.

Yes, but the observed, too, is wrong. One, after another, how blue is the difference in the eye of things.

How, to think how, if the hand is wrong?

"The distance not intended captures the oblique" : impossible, but for the distance in the error.

Unmoved, we have exhausted the air, although it's possible
as well to exclude a world inappropriate to optics.

This points to the disparity between the first minutes of each, although

here, too, we notice a resolution confined to material affairs.

Multitude is a noun, a study of the verb that declines to sing
in multitudes.

Figure the pieces needed – i.e. water, then water, with no sense
of the occasion.

Not yet summer, when it will be less than scene: i.e. this autonomous
product of its shape.

Then to continue, in conclusion, coming from these which are only
here. A grammar of the scene. Rust-colored little ones, at length.

In my argument I'd answer with this problem, that in all skies,
the covered roof runs to cloud the end with bricks.

"Still undetermined, it radiates the phrase as it is," he writes down,
reading. We believed in something, yes.

Clouds, to be, enlarged the roof. Others that are not, and
no one. What liberates, a case of ends: lacking terms, what impounds
the page. So noted, the rules had determined,
another one in that.

You and the world, whatever the return. This type, this
incline, neither of ascent nor certain flood. We omit
the leeward steps.

The question is when you should have asked. "When you've gone through, when you're in the country."

"*When my watch climbs down its adverbial brace.*"

The question follows, the upwards-in-direction, the "how do you like it," and the already understood. Here, as the manner may — although,

if the line drifts for no reason, it is likely out of deference to where again to travel. The next gives its cue along the line beneath:

thought for thought, the water speaks, interchangeably, to answer,

whereas the water speaks, interchangeably. The answer has been thought for thought.

To begin is to drift,

to remember the form you lose when, as drift,

the sea is unthinkable. If the wave is everywhere, the wave
is everywhere.

Look for direction, either in the winnow of coarse green, or for where
or when it left us. And for continuous vantage, a point in that law of
encoded image.

And as far as how to keep yourself, the diameter of one –
if it is to remain here by such lights, no ill-judged figure is more than
every line and word of the material involved, no more the answer to the
shadow the trees recover.

My portmanteau, after I stand by the door, to see the world. Because I think myself exhumed upon the sea. In the morning, it was. What do you call these trees?

But I stop myself – a long explication, I am estranged. But I demand to stop the moment. There is a right box and a wrong
box. I've read all the books of "Paradise Lost." A circle of
madrone and strawberries, monotone circle round the basin.

You said it, and they had some time to translate. I thought
they were water. One can listen, just for a little sympathy, as
now extended to work with *use*. Wide-eyed. And rain, or, more
rain, pending, this wave

just waiting. Who are immediately received by wave? Well, we always
say, "the verdict of the court." Or that neutral should be extended.
When were you a stretch of clear grain?

"The answer has more to do with things, with the knowledge
that the sea could be generated." On the other hand, a sea is
not the other hand.

The palm, so strong, and so diverse, and often lifeless.

What to hear when each cluster is a collection of point for point?
A complexity of zeroes, our request for anyone still within our range.

"Or every version of every one present, the savant in the scene's rapid
trial, the ending of the solitaire's parallel to sea?"

Would we ever come upon a word so misspelt, so as to say that either
the sweep of the pendulum or the swing of the planet . . .

There is, however, something that makes us conscious of complete arrest

Organum, récit, together, and together, in order

to say what is in this regard.

A coast, like every other, allowed to dry and set.

Against the dried edges of the sea,
the contour the ocean formed in each

and dried upon the hard form

the shore, like all boundaries, as the range of these
admissions.

About the Author

Steven Salmoni has published a previous chapbook, *Landscapes, With Green Mangoes* (Chax Press, 2011). Individual poems have appeared in journals such *Nerve Lantern, Fact-Simile, N/A, Spinning Jenny, Versal, Sonora Review*, and *Bombay Gin*, and a selection of his work was also included in the anthology *The Literary Field Guide to the Sonora Desert* (U of Arizona Press, 2016). The majority of his critical/scholarly work has focused on Henry James, specifically with regard to his travel writings and to the "international theme" in his fiction, and he has published articles on these subjects in *Studies in Travel Writing, The Journal of Narrative Theory* and *The Critical Companion to Henry James*. More recently, he has been studying modern and contemporary experimental poetry, often with regard to its relationship to phenomenology, poststructuralism and critical theory. In 2012, he contributed the article "Spectres Of Benjamin": (Re)Presentation And (Re)Semblance In Charles Bernstein's *Shadowtime*" to the *Salt Companion to Charles Bernstein*.

He lives in Tucson, Arizona, where he directs the Writing and Literature Programs at Pima College's Northwest Campus and serves as the Department Head for Communication Programs. He has been one of the directors of the poetry and art presentation nonprofit organization POG, Inc., for nine years.

About Chax

Founded in 1984 in Tucson, Arizona, Chax has published more than 240 books in a variety of formats, including hand printed letterpress books and chapbooks, hybrid chapbooks, book arts editions, and trade paperback editions such as the book you are holding. From August 2014 until July 2018 Chax Press resided in Victoria, Texas, where it was located in the University of Houston-Victoria Center for the Arts. UHV has supported the publication of Since I Moved In, which has also received support from friends of the press. Chax is a nonprofit 501(c)(3) organization which depends on support from various government private funders, and, primarily, from individual donors and readers In July 2018 Chax Press returned to Tucson, Arizona, while maintaining an affiliation with the University of Houston-Victoria. Our current address is 1517 North Wilmot Road no. 264, Tucson, Arizona 85712-4410. You can email us at chaxpress@gmail.com.

Recent books include *Rechelesse Pratticque* by Karen Mac Cormack, *The Hero* by Hélène Sanguinetti (transl. by Ann Cefola), *Since I Moved In* by Trace Peterson, *For Instance* by Eli Goldblatt, *Towards a Menagerie* by David Miller, *The Long White Cloud of Unknowing* by Lisa Samuels, and *Io's Song* by Murat Nemet-Nejat.

You may find CHAX at https://chax.org/